AF824442

Since You Won't Go to Counseling

5 Keys to a Better You!

By

Corey D. Sturdivant, D.Min

Foreword by Shawn R. Hutchinson

Since You Won't Go to Counseling

Published by Champions Leadership Institute

Clarksville, TN

In loving memory of my father… till we meet again.

FOREWORD

There are moments in life when a voice enters the room, and you instantly know it carries both weight and wisdom. A voice shaped not only by education or experience, but by compassion, conviction, and a deep desire to see people become the healthiest, truest version of themselves.

That voice belongs to my friend, my brother, Dr. Corey D. Sturdivant.

This book, Since You Won't Go to Counseling: Five Keys to a Better You, is not just a collection of ideas. It is a mirror. A challenge. A courageous invitation to confront the parts of ourselves we often avoid — our words, our relationships, our faith, our love, our purity, and ultimately... our identity.

Dr. Sturdivant has a rare ability to blend scholarship with soul. He speaks as a counselor, a believer, a teacher, a thinker, and a servant, but most importantly, as someone who genuinely cares about people becoming whole. In these pages, he does what many of us desperately need but rarely seek out. Dr. Sturdivant brings counseling to the reader, right where they are.

This book speaks to the conversations we avoid having with ourselves.

It wrestles with the power of speech and self-talk, how the words we speak shape the direction of our lives. It confronts how we communicate with others, how we interpret the world around us, and how culture influences our thinking and behavior. He guides us back to truth, back to responsibility, and back to purpose.

Dr. Sturdivant leans into topics many people shy away from — faith, love, identity, sexuality, benevolence, and purity — not from a place of judgment, but from a place of clarity and love. He writes with honesty, courage, and grace, challenging us not simply to believe better... but to be better.

What I respect most is that this book doesn't talk at you — it walks with you.

It doesn't condemn.
It doesn't preach from a distance.
It doesn't hide behind theory.

Instead, it walks into the real places of real people — the broken rooms, the silent battles, the unspoken doubts — and says:

"You matter. Your healing matters. Your wholeness matters. And your transformation begins now."

Dr. Sturdivant has written a work that is timely, necessary, and deeply relevant to the world we live in today. These five keys are not just principles — they are pathways. If you read this book with an open heart and a willing spirit, you will not leave the same way you entered.

I am honored not only to endorse this work, but to stand proudly beside the man who wrote it. A friend. A leader. A thinker. A servant of God. A brother whose life reflects what he teaches.

To every reader holding this book in your hands...

Take a breath.
Take your time.
Lean into the words.

Allow yourself to be challenged.
Allow yourself to be stretched.
Allow yourself ...finally ... to heal.

Your transformation begins on the next page.

Shawn R. Hutchinson
Serial Entrepreneur, Author, Life Coach

Introduction

"You can be anything you want to be. You can do anything you want as long as you put your mind to it." These words have been spoken to me since I can remember. My mother began planting those seeds early to ensure they took root before any doubt or insecurities crept into my young mind. Yet, although she has transitioned from this life, I can still hear those words.

I mostly hear them when I am facing a challenge or an obstacle in my life, ministry, or career. I hear them when considering a new endeavor. I hear them when I'm inspired by watching others succeed or when I'm thinking about doing something that has never been done before. I believed those words then. I still believe them now. I do not know if my mother gave this same speech to my siblings. I've never heard any of them mention it. I hope they've heard it before. If not, I hope they are reading it now.

In 2003, I became a father to a baby boy. In 2005, my beautiful daughter was born, and I became a father of two. The moment my wife, Jennifer, told me she was pregnant, I knew that I wanted to be a better man. I wanted to be a great father. Good was not enough. I had already learned from Jim Collins that "good is the enemy of great."[1] So, I did everything within my power to provide my children with love, discipline, order, and structure.

Today, with one child serving his country in the military and a daughter in her third year of college, let me tell you that Jen and I are proud parents of two adult children who have heard the same words their entire lives that I heard from my mother. You can be anything you want to be, and you can do whatever you set your mind to. I pray they believe, just as I do.

This book is written with my children in mind, but it is not just for them. As a pastor and counselor, I have coached, mentored, and helped people achieve goals they never thought possible. Some of the people I coached come from healthy homes with strong support systems, while others report a past they felt they had to escape. Alcoholism, toxic family members, and physical or mental abuse have been obstacles to overcome, but so have entitlement, racism, and narcissism.

Social scientists, philosophers, theologians, and psychologists have extensively debated the nature-versus-nurture question. If you are new to the discussion, I'll explain. Nature refers to the genetic influences on behavior, while nurture encompasses environmental factors. In other words, you are the way you are because you were born with certain proclivities, or you were taught to think and behave

---

[1] Jim Collins, *Good to Great: Why Some Companies Make the Leap... and Others Don't* (HarperCollins Publishers Inc., 2001), 1.

the way you do by your parents, peers, and situations that have influenced you over time.

Jay Adams argues, "Christian counselors do not have to wonder about the issue." He adds, "God has already changed the orientation of the Christian's nature by quickening him (i.e., by giving him spiritual life."[2] In essence, since God has changed the Christian's nature through his redeeming work, the believer only needs nurturing to become the best possible version of himself.

In 1 Timothy 4:12, Paul provides his protégé a short list of things that require nurturing for him to be effective in ministry. The New International Version translates it this way: Don't let anyone look down on you because you are young, but set an example for the believers in speech, in conduct, in love, in faith and in purity.[3]

This verse holds a special place in my heart. Jen and I taught it to our children, and when we became children and youth pastors, we instilled it into other people's children. Twenty years later, my children and many of the others we taught can still recite this verse quicker than they can recall John 3:16! Still, it is not enough to recite scripture. The goal is for us to live it.

---

[2] Jay E. Adams, "Nature/Nurture," in *The Practical Encyclopedia of Christian Counseling* (Cordova, TN: Institute for Nouthetic Studies, 2020), 129.

[3] *The New International Version* (Grand Rapids, MI: Zondervan, 2011), 1 Ti 4:12.

This book has been written to encourage you to be the person God has created you to be, guiding you through the five characteristics of a good disciple that the apostle Paul shared with Timothy. I suppose you could call them ancient secrets to success, if you want to sound particularly profound. We will refer to them as the five keys to a better you. I like the idea of keys because they imply the power to unlock doors in your life that may have been closed and previously inaccessible.

I hope to give them to you so that you can unlock your potential for greatness in every area of your life. We will discuss how mastering your speech will improve relationships. We will also discuss conduct and its intricate connection to achieving goals. You will learn that love is a choice, not just a feeling. I will show you the importance of activating faith to catapult you into your dreams. Finally, we will discuss purity by exploring your motive to be better.

The Concise Oxford English Dictionary defines self-help as the action or faculty of using one's own efforts and resources to achieve something, or provide for oneself, with little or no assistance from others.[4] This is not a self-help book. I believe we were all created to live in community for several reasons.

First, community helps us become the best versions of ourselves. I may not realize I have a problem with

---

[4] "Self-Help, n. Meanings, Etymology and More | Oxford English Dictionary," accessed September 12, 2025, https://www.oed.com/dictionary/self-help_n.

jealousy or covetousness until I meet someone who possesses a skill, ability, wealth, or something else I wish I had or think I deserve. Community reveals our strengths and our weaknesses. Community helps us see where we are. It is the starting point for where we want to go.

Second, community provides us with opportunities to grow by fostering an environment that encourages us to be our best selves for others. The best version of ourselves is most realized by our ability to meet others' needs. What good is a diamond nobody can see? Jesus put it this way – "You are the light of the world. A town built on a hill cannot be hidden. Neither do people light a lamp and put it under a bowl. Instead they put it on its stand, and it gives light to everyone in the house. In the same way, let your light shine before others, that they may see your good deeds and glorify your Father in heaven." [5]

There are many reasons why community is vital to our existence, but the two we have discussed are critical to our journey. To be sure, this is not a self-help book because helping yourself requires community. Thus, I encourage you to find a friend to read this book with and hold you accountable for putting into practice what you learn from it. Perhaps starting a group would be an even greater impact. The size of the group doesn't matter. What matters is that you are part of a community of believers who are

[5] *The New International Version* (Grand Rapids, MI: Zondervan, 2011), Mt 5:14–16.

committed to helping you become the best version of you that you desire to be.

Are you ready? Let's go!

Chapter 1: Speech

My son joined the United States Army after two years of college. It wasn't long before he was deployed to Bulgaria. Although he had dreams of being in the military at an early age, he was not adjusting well to living on his own. He experienced frequent bouts of depression, feelings of rage, and extreme dissatisfaction with his decision to join the armed forces.

One of his most significant challenges was his social life. He wasn't interested in the activities and conversations that young military men are typically stereotyped for. He's not a heavy drinker, and he has a high regard for women. He felt that his unit lacked competent leadership and that it was difficult to find appropriate mentorship and growth opportunities. In short, my son seemed unable to find his tribe, and this was an ongoing conversation for his first two years in the military.

Although we tried diligently, my wife and I ran out of words and ways to console him. One day, I suggested that we start reading a proverb a day together whenever he was able to call home. It didn't solve all of his perceived problems, but our calls often ended with more laughter than complaints about life downrange. One of our favorite quotes came from Proverbs 18:6-7. It reads, "The lips of fools bring them strife, and their mouths invite a beating. The mouths of fools are their undoing, and their lips are a snare to their very lives."[6]

We laugh at this verse every time we read it because, not only does it put people in our minds who we'd love to give a good thrashing, but it reminds us that when we are not careful with our own words, we bring undo challenges into our lives. In Dale Carnegie's book How to Win Friends and Influence People, Carnegie recounts a conversation at a dinner party in which a man quoted William Shakespeare but mistakenly attributed the quote to the Bible.

> I was attending a banquet one night given in Sir Ross's honor; and during the dinner, the man sitting next to me told a humorous story which hinged on the quotation "There's a divinity that shapes our ends, rough-hew them how we will." The raconteur mentioned that the quotation was from the Bible. He was wrong. I knew that. I knew it positively. There couldn't be the slightest doubt about it. And so, to get a feeling of importance and display my superiority, I appointed myself as an unsolicited and unwelcome committee of one to correct him. He stuck to his guns. What? From Shakespeare? Impossible! Absurd! That quotation was from the Bible. And he knew it.

[6] *The New International Version* (Grand Rapids, MI: Zondervan, 2011), Pr 18:6–7.

The storyteller was sitting on my right; and Frank Gammond, an old friend of mine, was seated at my left. Mr. Gammond had devoted years to the study of Shakespeare. So the storyteller and I agreed to submit the question to Mr. Gammond. Mr. Gammond listened, kicked me under the table, and then said: "Dale, you are wrong. The gentleman is right. It is from the Bible." On our way home that night, I said to Mr. Gammond: "Frank, you knew that quotation was from Shakespeare." "Yes, of course," he replied, "Hamlet, Act Five, Scene Two. But we were guests at a festive occasion, my dear Dale. Why prove to a man he is wrong? Is that going to make him like you? Why not let him save his face? He didn't ask for your opinion. He didn't want it. Why argue with him? Always avoid the acute angle." The man who said that taught me a lesson I'll never forget. I not only had made the storyteller uncomfortable, but had put my friend in an embarrassing situation. How much better it would have been had I not become argumentative.[7]

While Mr. Carnegie did not receive a beating that night, he certainly did not acquire a new friend. Nevertheless, Carnegie's story reinforces Proverbs 18:6-7. That is, we need to be selective with our word choices because they are vital to every stage of relationships. What

---

[7] Dale Carnegie, *How to Win Friends and Influence People*, Kindle (Simon & Schuster, n.d.).

a parent says to their toddler matters greatly. A teenager's self-esteem can be built up or destroyed by the words spoken by their peers. One's word choice on a first date will often be the deciding factor on whether they get a second date. Marriages are sustained and maintained, in large part, by words. Words also tear couples apart.

It's no wonder Scripture places such emphasis on words. Consider how the use of words deceived Eve in the Garden of Eden. Aaron and Miriam's words about Moses angered God, and a sickness came upon them, but Moses's words to God cured them. Esau's words cost him his birthright, and Joseph's words saved the lives of thousands of people when the Pharaoh listened to him.

Words are powerful enough to talk ourselves into great things or talk ourselves out of them. They have the power to encourage us to chase and realize our dreams. But they also have the power to prophesy our experiences into living nightmares.

I once heard someone say, "Always expect the worst. If you get the worst, you aren't surprised. If things work out, you will get more than you ever dreamed." I told them that was the absolute worst advice I have ever heard. It felt like a defeatist mentality. It sounds dark and miserable, with the potential to deter hopes, crush dreams, and destroy ambition. Unfortunately, I couldn't change this person's mind, and I witnessed him live a life of mediocrity for years. The words he spoke to himself had the power to push people away because when he convinced himself that everyone would hurt or betray him, he treated them as though they already had. When the relationships became rocky or ended, he acted as if it didn't bother him, because he was already expecting it.

Kotesky describes self-fulfilling prophecy as "a prediction or belief that serves to bring about its own fulfillment whereby the person believing it acts in such a way as to make the prophesied event more likely." He further explains, "People who believe they can produce only a little do so, while those who think they can do more actually do more. People taking surveys find the results they expect to find, influencing the responses. Hypnotists find that their success in hypnotizing a given person depends on whether or not they believe the person can be hypnotized. Psychotherapists have greater success if they believe the client can be helped."[8]

Self-Talk

Let's revisit an ancient story that has captivated audiences for centuries. It is the curious case of an elderly couple, Abram and Sarai. It is a curious case because after receiving a divine prophecy, Abram laughed at God's word. According to Moses, God told Abram that he would bless Abram and surely give him a son by Sarai, his wife. Abram

---

[8] R. L. Koteskey, "Self-Fulfilling Prophecy," in *Baker Encyclopedia of Psychology & Counseling*, ed. David G. Benner and Peter C. Hill, Baker Reference Library (Grand Rapids, MI: Baker Books, 1999), 1088.

responds to this word by falling to his knees and engaging in some self-talk.

"Abraham fell facedown; he laughed and said to himself, "Will a son be born to a man a hundred years old? Will Sarah bear a child at the age of ninety?" (Genesis 17:17)

It's important to emphasize here that this word was given to Abram directly from God. But the plot thickens, and here is a spoiler alert. In case you haven't read their story, you might want to put this book down and start reading Genesis 16 through 18. Otherwise, here goes the next part of the story. According to Moses, Abram and Sarai would hear this promise of a son again in quick succession, with three things to note:

1. The first time Abram heard the prophecy, it was between him and God (see Gen 17:1).
2. The second time, God apparently brought witnesses (see Gen 18:1)
3. The first time Abram laughed. The second time, Sarai laughed.

These three points are important to note because, while self-talk is powerful, words in the company of witnesses create a sense of accountability. Public words can be dangerous. They can incite crowds, raise armies, and spark wars. Or they can calm emotions, foster peaceful discourse, and help people reach mutually beneficial agreements.

Notice the difference in Abram's response between the first and second time he heard the promise. Again, the first time he laughs in doubt. The second time, there is no indication that he did so. Is it possible that Abram understood that the witnesses were something of a guarantee that God would do what he promised? Let's say that Abram may have wondered if he missed God. Using our imagination here, perhaps what Abram thought he heard God say was only wishful thinking. We've all done that before, right?

But this time, it's not just God and Abram. There are witnesses to the promise. Surely God is no liar. So, Abram is more than ever confident that what has been promised will come to pass. But Sarai laughed, and although her words were said only to herself, God heard her.

Then the Lord said to Abraham, "Why did Sarah laugh and say, 'Will I really have a child, now that I am old?' Is anything too hard for the Lord? I will return to you at the appointed time next year, and Sarah will have a son." Sarah was afraid, so she lied and said, "I did not laugh." But he said, "Yes, you did laugh." (Genesis 18:13-15)

Those who know the story might be thinking, "Self-talk did not keep them from the promise." This is true. Several reasons can be argued here. One could point out that self-fulfilling prophecies, also known as the Rosenthal effect, occurred in only one of three research studies, giving Sarai a greater chance of succeeding. Alternatively, one could argue that God's word is more powerful than any mere human word or thought, and despite her self-talk, God has the final say.

Something should be said about Abram's error, however. You may have noticed that Moses gave no indication in the text that Abram ever told his wife about the promised child. If this is the case, we should not be surprised that Sarai laughed. You'll recall that laughter was her husband's initial response when he heard it for the first time. In any case, Abram's neglect might indicate a communication problem between this couple.

With that said, let's return to Paul's letter to Timothy. As we have already established, Paul instructs his young protégé to be an example to believers in speech. We have already seen the importance of self-talk. We will now turn our attention to communication in relationships. We know that not all relationships are romantic ones. A father would not talk to his children the way he would speak to his spouse. Friends might engage in deep conversation, but keep the relationship strictly platonic. Myriad situations require the right style and type of communication. But, in light of what we have witnessed with Adam and Eve, Abram and Sarai, it seems fitting to address the issues surrounding communication in marriage.

Interpersonal Communication

Some people say they want to improve a relationship, but they sabotage this goal with poor communication habits. We now turn our attention to Dr. John Gottman's Four Horsemen of the Relationship Apocalypse, which helps us recognize the communication styles we practice that are scientifically proven to harm relationships. These horsemen are criticism, defensiveness, contempt, and stonewalling. Tim Clinton and John Trent summarize them this way.

> Criticism: is sometimes packaged as a question that implies the other person has a character flaw: "Why do you always do that? You never do what you say you're going to do. This is just another example of how I can't count on you for anything."
>
> Defensiveness. When we receive criticism, it's easy to retaliate with counter-criticism: "What do you mean I never do what I say? What about the dishes? Is that all you can do, whine and complain?
>
> Contempt. When criticism and defensiveness are ratcheted up several notches, they can lead to derogatory remarks, put-downs, and extreme disrespect. Not mowing the grass can lead to "You make me sick! You never do what you say you'll do. I'll just do everything myself."
>
> Stonewalling. When the intensity becomes too strong, a person can shut down and decide not to participate in the conversation. This would, understandably,

drive the other spouse crazy, intensifying rage and setting up the battle for another round of criticism.[9]

All four communication failures point to one thing: we devalue what God has valued. And when we do that, we are walking in deliberate sin. Jesus reminds us how important it is to value others in John 13:34. He says, "A new command I give you: Love one another. As I have loved you, so you must love one another."

Whenever I teach about love, I always emphasize that love meets needs. I add that love is a choice made evident by action. It is not so much a feeling as it is a decision. Thus, when we consider Jesus' command in John 13:34, we must wrestle with the fact that we are commanded to love one another as Jesus loves us. He saw our greatest need and started there. His words and actions aligned in a way that communicated the depth of his love.

I enjoy counseling couples struggling with communication problems because this challenge can be easily overcome. Many couples have learned poor communication styles from parents, friends, and leaders at work or from church, whom they respect. This phenomenon is known as the "halo effect."

The halo effect occurs when people assume that someone is equally competent in one area as in others. Advertisers who use athletes to promote their products are relying on the halo effect to persuade consumers to purchase their sports attire. The athlete may know little about shoe or

---

[9] The Quick-Reference Guide to Marriage & Family Counseling, *The Quick-Reference Guide to Marriage & Family Counseling*, Baker, 95–96.

equipment design, but the halo effect is activated because consumers assume athletes understand what people need to run faster or jump higher.

Politicians publicize endorsements from celebrities who may know nothing about politics. Because they are popular and award-winning actors or singers, people often agree with their endorsements and vote for the candidate they support. This is the power of the halo effect. It is challenging to convince people to abandon a model they learned from someone they admire, so I often ask couples to communicate their ideal marriage. We might use a vision board or a five-year plan to reveal ideas and plans that have not been previously communicated. This work often reveals that the person may not honestly want their marriage to resemble the one they've been admiring. It helps them see how the halo effect has skewed their perception, and it gets them back on track.

Communication in marriage requires couples to purge. By purge, I mean patience, understanding, reassurance, grace, and encouragement (P.U.R.G.E.). Not all individuals are raised in the same circumstances. A couple might discover that, although they grew up in a two-parent home, their partner grew up in a single-parent home. One person saw their parents argue daily, while the other never heard their parents raise their voice. Thus, purging serves a two-fold purpose. It reminds couples to consider multiple elements of effective communication while simultaneously eliminating historical models that do not benefit their relationship. The details of the acrostic are as follows:

1. Patience: No one is perfect. People and things change. Couples who exercise patience with one another allow room for growth. Because life is lived in stages, we need to be patient with one another as we learn to adapt to the new stages as they arrive.
2. Understanding: Communication is a two-way street. Just because a message is transmitted doesn't mean it is received as intended. To understand one another, couples need to decode the message's meaning properly, with the assumption that intentions are well-meaning.
3. Reassurance: Safety is essential to any healthy relationship. In communication, couples need reassurance that they will not be judged for their feelings or word choices when expressing their feelings or viewpoints.
4. Grace: Again, no one is perfect. When we express our feelings or thoughts, we may fall short of the right words. Some of the things we say may come across as offensive, even when we don't mean to. Giving your partner the benefit of the doubt goes a long way in improving communication.
5. Encouragement: The best way to encourage open communication is to be attentive, show empathy, practice active listening, and withhold judgment while your partner is speaking. Rephrasing their words to show understanding and affirming their right to their opinion encourages open communication.

We are always communicating. It is true that when we don't talk things out, we tend to act them out. The problem with acting things out is that it leaves too much room for incorrect interpretation. If you desire to have a marriage that lasts, practice purging as you communicate and avoid the four horsemen of the relationship apocalypse as much as possible.

I don't believe it's necessary to tell you that all of the above is true for platonic relationships, as well. However, for the sake of my own conscience, I want to encourage you to take a few cues from Dale Carnegie. Here are three of my favorites:

1. "You can make more friends in two months by becoming interested in other people than you can in two years by trying to get other people interested in you.[10]
2. The only way to get the best of an argument is to avoid it.[11]
3. Criticism is futile because it puts a person on the defensive and usually makes them strive to justify themselves.[12]

God created us to live in a harmonious, interdependent community. See Genesis 2:18. The only way to maintain unity is through communication. Let's examine communication on a broader scale and see

[10] Carnegie, *How to Win Friends and Influence People*, 91.
[11] Carnegie, *How to Win Friends and Influence People*, 182.
[12] Carnegie, *How to Win Friends and Influence People*, 195.

what we can learn when it breaks down. To this end, we will consider a familiar story – the Tower of Babel.

Mass Communication

In Genesis 11, Moses explains how people who spoke the same language established a city together and decided to build a tower. This tower was supposed to reach heaven and somehow avoid any chances of scattering. Obviously, this is problematic because from the beginning, God's command to humanity was to fill the earth and subdue it. See Genesis 1:28. But the people were committed to doing things their way, instead of doing it God's way.

Moses tells us that the Lord observed their actions and decided to confuse their language, causing them to stop building and scatter across the earth. While there are a plethora of theological topics that can be extracted from this text, following those arguments is outside of the scope of this conversation. What I want you to see is the power of good communication. According to the Genesis text, God saw that nothing would be impossible for these people if they could communicate effectively, so he confused their language to get them back on track with his plan.

Imagine what would have happened if, instead of committing to disobeying God, the people had committed to filling and subduing the earth together. Is it possible that many of today's issues, such as nationalism, territorial feuds, and wars, would have never existed if people communicated and accepted God's plan over their own? Perhaps the issue of race and culture would be nonexistent. Instead, this great sin of disobedience rears its ugly head. This time, it is bigger than the disobedience of one man and his wife in a garden. The sin of Babel impacts the world.

The Tower of Babel serves as a reminder that a leader's communication to the masses can have severe consequences or excellent positive results. Knowing this, Paul teaches Timothy to be exemplary in his public communication just as he is in his private communication. Paul is holding Timothy accountable and expects his public speech to be seasoned with wisdom.

Throughout history, our world has witnessed how a person's words can shape the world. From those who publicly shouted, "Crucify him," to those who shouted, "Hail Hitler," From "We shall overcome," to "Black Lives Matter," and everything in between, our public proclamations will be considered the day we stand before the King of kings and Lord of lords. Jesus told his disciples that everyone will have to give an account on the day of judgment for every empty word they have spoken. See Matthew 12:36-37. Paul wants to ensure that Timothy's account is good and pleasing to God on that great day. I want that for you, as well.

We have discussed the importance of communication, from self-talk to corporate or mass communication. We have learned that our speech can influence us to talk ourselves into or out of various things, such as goals, plans, and even relationships. We considered the power of speech in marriage and public settings, and we learned that God holds us accountable for every word we speak, especially the words that do not add value.

In the next chapter, we will address what it means to live an exemplary life as a believer. We will explore concepts like integrity, service, and excellence. We will read stories that help us understand that God does not expect us to be perfect, but he does expect us to be consistent and to depend on the power of the Holy Spirit to help us be what we cannot be on our own.

Chapter 2: Conduct

I separated from the U.S. Air Force in 2009 and began working for the State of Tennessee shortly after. Unhappy with my career and unsure of what to do next, I vented my frustrations to my father. He did not know what to say, but he did the next best thing. He gave me a CD that he picked up while visiting Mt. Zion Baptist Church in Nashville. Bishop Joseph W. Walker III had recently taught a lesson entitled, "How to Make Good Decisions." While sitting in my car at a park in Nashville during my lunch break, I listened to the sermon. The line that has stuck with me for more than ten years after hearing it was Bishop Walker's: "Your current situation in life is the result of a series of choices you've made over your lifetime."

That was it. It was exactly what I needed to hear to eliminate all of my excuses. That line freed me from the victim mentality. It taught me that I could reinvent myself at any moment if I were committed to becoming who I wanted to be. I learned that in five years or less, my life can change and not by the grace or mercies of others, but by the choices I make daily, weekly, and annually. I started applying that lesson to my life and over the next five years, I earned a Master's degree in Religion, wrote and published my first book, changed careers, and nearly tripled my income. It is safe to say that, thanks to God's providence and my commitment to making decisions that align with my goals, I am currently living a life that far exceeds my expectations.

I once heard Andy Stanley say something to the tune of, "Discipline, not desire, leads to your destination." This quote serves as an excellent reminder that life is not entirely about chance or luck. We are not as powerless as we think. We are more powerful than we are typically comfortable admitting. The life we experience is very much in our control. Thus, Paul adds this order to the list of things Timothy must exemplify.

"Be an example to the believer in speech, in conduct..." 1 Timothy 4:12

Shortly after my son's twenty-second birthday, I gave him my dream car. It was a 2015 Dodge Challenger SRT 392 with a 6.4-liter Hemi V8 engine. That equates to 485hp and 475 lb.-ft of torque. Because he had never driven a manual transmission, he had to learn to drive it in two days if we were going to take the planned road trip to get the car to El Paso, where the U.S. Army had stationed him. Previous learning experiences proved that my wife was the best option for teaching him, and she did a fantastic job preparing him for the journey.

I appreciate that he followed my advice and watched YouTube videos on driving a manual transmission weeks before the trip. I was convinced that these videos would mentally prepare him to learn as fast as possible. On the drive to El Paso, I was surprised by how well he drove, and the trip was enjoyable. The best part of the journey, however, was not his driving. It was the conversations we had along the way.

Like most healthy father-son relationships, we discussed cars, careers, politics, theology, and, of course, girls. Something in that conversation compelled me to confess to him that I intentionally did not teach him how to talk to girls during his adolescent and teenage years because I did not want him to grow into a womanizer. My son is handsome, tall, and muscular. He played football and wrestled, so you might understand my concerns.

Since it was amnesty hour, I also explained why I was so strict with him when he was young. I repeatedly told him that I would be his discipline until he developed self-discipline. I wanted to instill confidence, order, and bearing in him so that he would know how to conduct himself in various situations. He mentioned that although I was tough on him, he appreciated it because it helped him become the person he is today.

We recalled when he was in middle school, my wife received a call from the local police. It is always frightening to get a call from the police when your children are not home. This is especially true when your children are hanging out with friends you don't know very well. I was sitting next to her when her phone rang.

"Hello?"

"Yes, this is Officer Johnson from Brighton PD. May I speak to Mrs. Sturdivant?"

"This is she. How can I help you?"

"I'm calling because I'm here with your son."

My wife stood up nervously and asked, *"Is everything okay?"*

"Yes, ma'am. There was an incident at Taco Bell with a few minors."

My wife interrupted. *"Is Samuel okay?"*

"Well, that's what I'm calling about. I wanted you to know that you have raised a fine young man. He was on the scene when I arrived, and because of the situation, I had to interview a few of the kids here. He was so impressive in his speech, posture, and attitude that I had to let you know that this is a kid you can be proud of."

My wife sighed in relief. *"Oh, we are proud of him. Thanks for your call. I'm glad he's okay."*

"Yes, ma'am," the officer continued. He's the perfect example of what teenagers should be. He's clearly a leader, and I wish you all the best."

She thanked the officer for calling and immediately called my son's phone to tell him. We reminded him how character goes a long way. We also discussed the importance of presenting yourself in the best possible light. We reminded him how proud we were of him as he shared his side of the story.

Frederick Douglass is credited with saying, "It is easier to build strong children than to repair broken men." Research suggests that the best approach to building strong children is in a two-parent household where the mother and father are actively involved in the child's upbringing. According to Michael S. Horton, over 80% of adolescents in psychiatric hospitals come from broken families, approximately three out of four teenage suicides occur in households with an absent parent, and boys growing up without a father are at greater risk for learning impairments.[13]

In 1 Timothy 4:12, when Paul emphasizes conduct in his exhortation to Timothy, he undoubtedly has Timothy's mother and grandmother in mind, who, according to 2 Timothy 1:5, may have played a significant role in Timothy's development as a follower of The Faith. Indeed, a person's character develops from childhood and is arguably a result of grooming. Nurture is a vital element in the development of good conduct in children. Bad habits do indeed die hard, so parents must foster nurturing atmospheres that weed out bad habits and feed and affirm positive ones.

This is important for us to understand because some of us may have been raised in homes that did not provide the nurturing, education, or guidance necessary to develop good habits and positive behaviors. Perhaps your father was not there to teach you how to respond when people disrespect you. Your mother may have been a poor role model for relationships. Maybe you learned poor coping skills from your alcohol addicted uncle. Right now, you might see your life following the same patterns as those of the

---

[13] Michael S. Horton, *The Law of Perfect Freedom: Relating to God and Others through Teh Ten Commandments* (Moody Publisher, 1993), 191.

people who raised you, but you want more. You want better. Well, friend, it is never too late to turn your life around.

Take a moment and self-reflect. Are you living the life you've dreamed of? Have you ever dared to dream? Have you taken the steps necessary to make your dream a reality? What books are you reading? Who are you listening to? What are you watching that inspires, encourages, and equips you to reach your goals? The answers to all of these questions will determine whether you will ever live an exemplary life.

As Bishop Walker said, "Your current position in life is the result of a series of choices you have made over a lifetime." The good news is that you can start making new choices today that will alter the trajectory of your life. At any moment, you can change direction. You can change your influences. You can abandon your misguided upbringing. You can change how you think about and spend your time, talent, and treasure. It may not be easy, but it is simple.

What Did Jesus Say?

In our anchor text, Paul tells Timothy, "Don't let anyone look down on you because you are young, but set an example to the believers in speech and conduct (behavior, customs, or paradigms)..." If we were to compare Paul's teaching to what Jesus has to say on the matter, we know that Paul's advice is sound. In Matthew 6:33, Jesus says, "Seek first the Kingdom of God and his righteousness…"

Righteousness refers to the proper way of doing things. Thus, it could be read, "Seek first the kingdom of God and the right way of doing things, and all these things will be given to you as well." Some benefits come with righteous living, just like there are consequences that come with unrighteous living. We often blame the devil for the consequences that result from the choices we make, but we rarely blame him for the consequences that result in favorable results. We give ourselves the credit for that. Regardless of who you blame or credit, the fact is that when you make the right choices, the benefits typically follow.

If I were to ask you what is most important to you, what would you say if you were completely honest? If I were to inquire about your purpose in life, could you provide a statement of purpose? I'll ask another way: at the end of your life, what do you want people to say about you? What should they write right on your Tombstone?

"She made big money?"

"He was a smooth talker?"

What should they write on your Tombstone that would be truthful about you? We all have or will have to wrestle with the question: Why am I here? What is my purpose? The good news is that we don't have to guess that hard because Jesus told us to seek the kingdom of God and all its righteousness. That is the meaning of life, ladies and gentlemen. I'll gladly take my Nobel Peace Prize now.

The Meaning of Life

The meaning of life is to seek the kingdom of God and all of his righteousness. In other words, in every area of your life, the question that you should be asking yourself before you make any decision is, "Is this right with God? Before you cuss him out, "Is this right with God before you decide to never speak to them again, is that right with God?

I get it. As the saying goes, "it's easier said than done." It's easier to say you're a Christian than to actually be one. A lot of people say that Christianity is a crutch and it's for the weak. My question to those critics is always the same. Have you tried it? Then I tell them that the Faith walk is not as easy as they think. When you think of the hardships that many believers have endured, it isn't as much of a crutch as some assume. It's hard work to restrain when you want to give somebody a piece of your mind instead of the mind of Christ. It's challenging when you want to throw hands instead of lay hands.

On second thought, maybe it is a crutch because, without the love and power of God operating in our lives, some of us might have a domestic assault or two on our police records. Thank God for the crutch that has kept me from falling! Thank God for wisdom that keeps me from making the wrong choice in moments of temptation. You see, when we're faced with a decision, the question that must be answered is: Does this please God? Jesus says that if you seek it, then all the other things follow, provided they are in God's will and right with God.

Paul writes in Romans 12:1, "Therefore I urge you, brothers and sisters…" He's pressing this on you. It's so important. It is vital to your life and your purpose. He adds, "…in view of God's mercy…" That means you didn't get what you deserved for your evil deeds. That's mercy. Paul says, "In view of God's mercy, offer your bodies as a living sacrifice".

In ancient religious systems, when a person sacrificed something, the priest had to kill it before putting it on the altar. Whether it was a bull or a turtle dove, it had to die in order to be sacrificed. The good news is that God is not asking us to die because Jesus has already died for us. However, the least we can do is offer ourselves as living sacrifices – to be what God has called us to be, regardless of how it feels.

To offer our bodies as a living sacrifice is a holy act. Holy means different. Our sacrifice should also be acceptable or pleasing to God. Have you ever taken a moment to reflect on your day and look back on how it went, saying, 'I bet I made God smile today'? Most people don't. Let me encourage you to try living a whole day with an attitude that says, "I bet I'm about to make God smile." With every choice you face, tell yourself, "I'm about to make God smile." Before you eat a pound of bacon for breakfast tomorrow, ask yourself how God feels about it. Would it make God smile?

I want you to make good choices for breakfast, lunch, and dinner. Think about what you might wear on your next date. I'm not just talking about the ladies. Some brothers like to have all their taco meat out at parties. Put it away! You don't need your shirt open all the way down to the fourth button. Say it with me. "I'm about to make God smile!" Make that your mantra this week. Make God smile in your conversations.

"I urge you, brothers and sisters, in view of God's mercy to offer your bodies a living sacrifice, holy and pleasing to God. This is your true and proper worship."

Some translations read, "This is your reasonable service." Paul continues his letter by urging believers to refuse the temptation to conform to the pattern of this world. He writes, "but be transformed by the renewing of your mind." Paul is giving some insight into why it's so difficult to break bad habits. For Paul, it is because you still think the same way about those habits. You will never change your behavior as long as your thought pattern remains the same. However, by renewing your mind, you open yourself up to better decisions.

For instance, let's say you have a habit of overeating, and you keep telling yourself, "I'm quitting cake." You add, "I'm going to start working out five times a week." You know you're not. You're not even going to stop eating cake. Perhaps your words conveyed it, but your mind hasn't changed its stance on the matter. You'll find out at the next party you attend.

Some of us eat sweets when we're emotionally exhausted, and we find comfort in that. We don't work out because it's cold outside. Who wants to leave your home when you're all snuggled up in your blanket? We find any excuse to eat the cake and stay home. This sounds harsh, so how about we don't call it an excuse? Let's call it a reason because we know that excuses are crutches for the uncommitted. We know that people who master excuses master little to nothing else. So, let's say we don't make excuses. We have reasons. Unfortunately, your reasons won't help you meet your goals either.

Here's what will. Plans! Plans foster commitment and discipline. Commitment and discipline create a structure that disregards feelings. So, instead of saying, "I'm going to stop eating cake whenever I feel emotional," start saying, "I am going to be a healthy person." The next time you look at a cake, you can ask yourself if a healthy person would eat it. Then, make the decision based on the habits of a healthy person. This is called identity-based habits, and it works![14]

Seriously. I did it the morning I wrote this. I looked at the cupcakes sitting on the counter at home and asked my wife if she wanted breakfast. She asked what I had in mind. I said, "Well, I'm thinking about cupcakes and coffee." I was joking, unless she was okay with it. She was not. My wife helps me to avoid the wrong stuff most days. Besides, I had already decided that I wanted to be a healthy person. That made it easier for me to look at that cupcake and say, "I ain't eating that!" A healthy person would not eat that.

Maybe your problem is not cupcakes? Perhaps you're a known liar, and you want to break the habit. In that case, stop saying, "I'm going to stop lying." Instead, commit to being an honest person. Then, the next time someone tempts

---

[14] James Clear, *Atomic Habits: An Easy & Proven Way to Build Good Habits & Break Bad Ones* (Avery, 2018).

you with a conversation, and you have the tea, remind yourself who you are now. Can you see how this changes everything? Try it for three or four weeks. If I'm wrong, please reach out to me for a coaching session, and I'll do my best to help you iron this out. In the meantime, let's get back to the questions at hand: Why am I here? What does God want from me? What is my purpose? What is God's plan for my life?

I maintain that you can test God's plan for your life by offering your body as a living sacrifice. Refusing to conform to this world will change the way you think about things. This requires repentance. Repent means to change the way you think about things. It means to change the direction in which you were going. Repent means that I've changed my mind about what I used to think was okay, so that my thoughts align with God's thoughts about everything. This is how one can test God's good and perfect will. Should I punch him in the face or not? Test that against the word of God.

Christianity is not rocket science, but we make it so difficult sometimes. I once preached what I thought was the best sermon I had ever delivered. I was in my super suit that day until I read one of the comment cards, where a guest wrote, "We really enjoyed ourselves. The teaching was so basic and easy to understand." I felt some kind of way about that. What did he mean by basic? That was 30 hours of prep work. I poured my heart and soul into those pages and delivered the message well. I know. I'm my worst critic. So, I was offended by the comment. Later, I thought about it and told my wife, "You know, that's always been my goal anyway – to make preaching so simple that an 8-year-old can understand but so meaningful that a 71-year-old can say, 'Today's message changed my life."

Paul writes, "Then you'll be able to test and approve God's will. His good, pleasing, and perfect will." Some scholars argue that Paul is expressing the idea that there are three different wills. The argument is that there's a good will, a pleasing will, and a perfect will of God. I'm not sure if those are three distinct things or just synonyms for God's will. This discussion does not seem to be in Paul's mind, however. Scholars agree that Paul calls for the transformation of the mind because he knows that attitudes generate actions. Hoyt suggests, "This transformation is not a one-time event but a constant struggle. The Christian's agenda is not to be determined by the current secular standards".[15]

To be sure, the point is that we do not continue in activities and thoughts that are knowingly outside of God's will. We need to change our thinking. Once we change our perspective on something, we change our behavior. We act according to what we believe. We believe according to how we think. We think based on the information we expose ourselves to. This is why reading the word of God is so important. Once you believe scripture is more important than social media, textbooks, and popular opinion, your actions will follow.

---

[15] Thomas L. Hoyt, "Romans," in *True to Our Native Land: An African American New Testament Commentary*, ed. Brian K. Blount et al. (Minneapolis, MN: Fortress Press, 2007), 268.

Earlier, we touched on the litmus test that helps us test and approve the will of God. If the suspense added stress to your reading, let's relieve you with the first clause of this verse.

Galatians 5:19: "The acts of the Flesh…"

By "the flesh," Paul doesn't necessarily mean your physical body. He means your way of thinking that is contrary to the way God thinks. Humans are composed of two parts: the visible and the invisible. We are spiritual beings having an earthly experience. To have an earthly experience, we need a physical body made of flesh. Paul argues that the acts of the flesh are obvious. He lists them out in Galatians 5, beginning with sexual immorality.

Let's Talk About Sex

Now is not a bad time to go back to the basics. First, the whole purpose of sex is procreation. God made it feel good, so you want to do it. How else would we desire to multiply on the Earth? I often laugh at regular churchgoers because the three things they most want more of are usually taboo during most church gatherings. Apparently, people don't like to talk about power, money, and sex. People clam up when I talk about it. We become pious and proper, sometimes even pretending to be clueless about the birds and the bees. I once taught this at a church meeting, and the group's faces all said, "I don't want anything but to serve the Lord!" I was not convinced.

Paul writes, "The acts of the flesh are obvious sexual immorality, impurity,.debauchery, idolatry, and witchcraft." Interestingly, Paul had to address the issue of witchcraft while writing to the church. Perhaps they used tarot cards and burned sage, as some people do today. I'll go into more detail about this in a future book, but for now, you should know that none of those things are compatible with Christianity. By the way, idolatry is not necessarily about setting up a statue to worship. Unfortunately, some of us worship an idol and call it Jesus. What I mean is, you have created a Jesus that does not match the character of the Jesus we read about in the Bible. You have expectations of God that do not align with how God has revealed Himself.

Many people think God looks past sexual immorality, arguing from a post-Christian worldview that God has no opinion about sex before marriage. Yet, a proper study of Acts, Corinthians, Ephesians, Jude, and other New Testament books reveals that this is not true. Furthermore, sex outside of marriage often leads to spiritual and physical consequences, including guilt, shame, and in some cases, sexually transmitted diseases and domestic disputes.

Paul warns his readers about other conduct that disqualifies us from the kingdom inheritance before introducing the fruit of the Spirit in Galatians 5:22. According to Paul, there is no law against those virtuous characteristics. That is to say, when we conduct our lives after the manner of God's Holy Spirit, we are considered righteous before God and man. Brad R. Braxton contends, "The same Spirit who created and confirmed the Galatians' divine acceptance is also sufficient to guide their moral affairs".[16]

God's Version of You

This might be news to some and a reminder for others, but the best version of you will be the one closest to Jesus. That's not to say you aren't a good person, but you and I both know you could be better. None of us is perfect, but some of us know the perfect one, and the more we become like him, the better the world is for it. And here's why.

Christlikeness is only a reality in the midst of community. You only know you're selfish or generous by how you react to someone who's in need. You only know you're patient and kind when you're given an opportunity to be patient and kind to others. The best version of you will only be visible when you're in the company of others.

Do you have a vision of the best version of you yet? What does that look like? Who are their friends? What kind of impact does that version of you make in the world? Who is that person mentoring, and most importantly, what does God think of that version of you? These are vital questions because if your best version of yourself doesn't align with

---

[16] Brad R. Braxton, "Galatians," in *True to Our Native Land: An African American New Testament Commentary*, ed. Brian K. Blount et al. (Minneapolis, MN: Fortress Press, 2007), 344.

God's vision for you, you might spend an entire lifetime living in the less-than.

There was a time in my life when all I wanted was not to be poor. But God's vision for me was so much more than that. Some of you just wanted your own apartment, but God wants to give you a house on acres of land. Some of us just wanted to graduate high school, and now you're working on your master's or doctorate. God's vision for you includes the best version of you. In fact, that's his priority. Don't misunderstand this. What you have, the car you drive, the money you make, is not God's vision for you. That's his provision for you. His vision for you is a version of you. He provides what you need to support his vision of you, but he releases provision on an as-needed basis.

Some of us don't have what we want because we aren't doing anything with what we have. We have gifts and talents that we don't use. Skills and abilities that we downplay and even sometimes despise. By God's provision, we have everything we need to go to the next level, but we can't see it because we lack vision. How do I know? Because vision sets boundaries. It creates rules that determine direction. Vision says, 'Don't eat that sugar or drink that soda if you want a flat belly.' It says, Don't treat her that way if you want to keep her. Vision says finish the book, pay the bill on time, and show up for work even when you don't feel like it.

But without vision, God says, 'My people perish.' They cast off restraint. They have no boundaries, no guard rails. Until you see what God sees, you will cast off the provision of restraint. You will disregard wisdom and make decisions that contradict God's plan for your life. That's called DI-vision. Di means two. There are two visions at war with each other, yours and God's.

We like to pretend we don't know what God's voice sounds like. Here's a clue next time you're confused. The devil will never tell you to share Jesus with someone. The devil isn't telling you to help the old racist neighbor with their yard. He's not telling you to feed the homeless. That's the voice of the savior. So, the next time you feel led to do that, you know you're hearing God. The more you obey him with things that help others, the More you'll get used to hearing and knowing his voice. Notice the examples I just gave impact people beyond you. Again, God created us to live in community.

My wife loves to travel, but before she goes anywhere, she does thorough research. She reads everything she can get her hands on about the location. She studies what people have said about it and weeds out the sources that don't appear credible. Based on what she learns about the destination, she makes detailed plans that include what clothes to bring, where she will stay, what she will eat and where, and what sites she plans to see. That's vision.

However, vision without motion is nothing more than a daydream. She still has to get in a car, or plane, or boat; she needs a mode of transportation to get her from what she read about to what she wants to be about. What would happen if she got off the plane and arrived at her hotel, only to find that no one was there? What would her trip be like if she went to the restaurant she researched, and the chef didn't show up? If the museum employees slept in and the tour guide decided on a new career the day she arrived, what would she have to say about that location? Is that the best it has to offer?

Here's the point: God's vision for the best version of us requires three things:

1. It requires the Word, the good news, the truth that we don't have to stay where we are. There is a place that God has prepared for us, one that includes a better version of ourselves than what we have been accustomed to. John tells us, 'In the beginning was the word, the word was God and was with God'. That word became flesh and dwelt among us. That word healed the sick and raised the dead. That word set the captives free. That word stretched his arms and hung on a cross to die for sins he didn't commit so that we could become who and what we haven't been. The best version of us needs the word.

2. The best version of us requires a vehicle that has the power to get us from where we are to where God wants us to be. That vehicle is the Holy Spirit, whom Jesus promised to his disciples to lead us into all truth. The Holy Spirit gives us power to walk right and talk right, to become sons and daughters of the Most High God. According to Peter, this promised Holy Spirit is a generational promise,

and as far as I can tell, it's a gift that just keeps giving. If you've got the Holy Spirit, pause for a moment and clap your hands. If you are in a public setting, snap your fingers instead, or tap your feet and say, 'Thank you, Lord, for the gift of the Holy Spirit!'

3. The best version of us requires a community to share the best versions of us so that when others get here, they experience the 'Oh taste and see' that the psalmist wrote about. What good is a great chef if no one ever tastes his food? What's the point of a beautiful voice no one gets to hear? Who benefits from a friendly smile that no one gets to see?

God's vision was to create man in His image and likeness, and to live with them in holy harmony. That vision came with provision, as He placed Adam and Eve in a beautiful garden, giving them dominion over every created thing and access to all they needed to live an abundant life. But Adam and Eve were enticed by a new vision, one that was separate from God's. That caused a division. But because God loved the world so much, he graciously provided a revision – a vision of you saved from the snare and trap of the enemy. A vision of you whole and restored. A vision of you walking in power and victory. Tell your neighbor you are a champion, and I see it all over you. There's a winner in your spirit. You are more than a conqueror. Lift your head, hold your shoulders back, and walk into your season of victory.

As we conclude, I want to remind you that God's vision for us included provision. Sin caused division among us, but love gave revision to us. And that's the good news. That God sent his only begotten Son to live out the vision of perfect humanity, to die in representation of all those who couldn't, to resurrect on behalf of those who couldn't in order to present to the Father, sons and daughters who could not present themselves. That is the gospel of Jesus Christ. As I said from the beginning, the best version of ourselves is the one closest to Jesus. I'm determined to draw near, and I hope you are too.

In the next chapter, we will talk about love. Guys, don't skip this chapter. It's not what you think. In fact, you might be relieved when you hear my description of love. Ladies, you might be surprised to discover that your partner is more loving than you give him credit for. Brace yourselves. The next chapter promises to be an enjoyable ride.

Chapter 3: Love & Benevolence

Let's begin this chapter with the facts. God is not expecting perfection, but availability, because God can make the best out of what is available. I believe the best human being is not the one who makes the most money or owns the biggest house. It's not the man or woman with the fanciest car or most attractive spouse. The best of us are the ones who extend the love of God in a way that makes others feel as though they are in the arms of God whenever they come in contact with the best of us.

In this chapter, I'd like to discuss a word that is underused and undervalued. It is also too often misunderstood. That word is benevolence. Benevolence is a fancy way to describe non-romantic love, but since the word's usage is somewhat antiquated, I'll interchange it with what is more familiar. To be sure, we're talking about love.

Love in Action

Booker T. Washington was born a slave, worked his way through college as a janitor, and founded Tuskegee Institute in Montgomery, AL. In his book, "Up from Slavery," Washington keenly noted, "Those who are happiest are those who do the most for others."[17]

I, too, have noticed in my lifetime that those who do for others seem to have more joy than those who appear

[17] Booker T. Washington, *Up From Slavery*, Dover Thrift Editions: Black History (Dover Publications, 1995).

selfish and narcissistic. You may have noticed in elementary school how the so-called teacher's pet always seems to have a pep in her step. Go to a high school football game and watch the water boy in action. If he's a good one, you might question why he's not suited up to run back kick returns. The maid of honor is rightly named as she tends to serve from a place of love. This love for her friend tends to drive the elite bride's maid to work harder than all the rest as she proves her love by meeting needs.

Consider the mother who seems to rarely sleep as she raises her children, the father who works multiple jobs to pay his children's college tuition. Years of labor should put wrinkles on their faces and exhaustion in their eyes. Still, when that child walks across that stage in exchange for his diploma, as the young lady accepts the ring placed on her finger, and at the end of the fourth quarter, those who served are as excited, if not more, for the accomplishments of the one who received the service.

When the team won, so did the water boy. When the marriage ceremony and reception go perfectly, does the maid of honor not get a feeling of accomplishment? Indeed, those who are the happiest are those who do the most for others. They are the ones who meet needs. They meet needs from a place of love. Love is, therefore, a choice that is made evident by action.

Love is a Choice Made Evident by Action

Love can be known to a child by his parent who cares for him. It can be known between a young couple who plan to spend their entire lives together. And love can be expressed even between two perfect strangers because love is a choice! Jesus gives us a perfect example of love in Luke 10:25-37. The passage reveals six people we should pay attention to in the hopes of learning a valuable life lesson.

First, there is the unknown victim. We do not know if the person is Jew or Gentile, young or old, rich or poor. Still, somehow in some way, many of us can identify with his situation. We've been robbed, if not physically, then mentally or emotionally, by people who have been reckless with our persons. We know what it's like to be a victim, although we don't want to be identified as one.

Second, we read about the unidentified perpetrators. Again, we are not told if they are Jew or Gentile, young or old, rich or poor, but we certainly don't want to see ourselves as they are. The unfortunate truth is that there is at least one person in the world who, according to their version of you, would testify that you are, in fact, the perpetrator of their pain. Which means we identify whether we want to or not.

Third, we learn of a priest. He is likely a Jewish priest over thirty years old. While he may not be rich, it is unlikely that he's poor. As a priest, his role is to represent God to the people and represent the people to God. He is an advocate, an ambassador of sorts, who serves the purpose of bridging the gap between heaven and earth. His purpose is to be an agent of reconciliation between a Holy God and fallen humanity, but his preferences got in the way of his assignment.

It is possible that he was headed somewhere to perform an official duty, perhaps because the Sabbath was approaching, and knowing the travel limitations, he did not want to be delayed. Surely God's work is of the utmost importance, and since he was headed to do just that, the priest felt no obligation to help him.

We all have our own prejudices and biases; we are all aware of people we wouldn't spit on if they were on fire. As ministers of the Gospel and church practitioners, we can't wait to preach, itching to shine as we sing our solos, and dying for a title that says we are called to do God's work. Yet, we don't want to be identified as being like this priest.

In fact, we're not priests. At least most of us are not. Sure, we volunteer at the church, where we teach the children and sing on the worship team; we might even greet people at the doors, but we don't do that priestly stuff. We're just here to help. Well, those helpers are called Levites. And Jesus includes them in this story as well.

Here we have the Levite. The scriptures help us understand who they are historically. Jesus's listeners can identify with the Levite, who is a Jew. He's relatively young, and since he is part of the tabernacle system, he's not exactly poor. This person is closer to home for them. He may not be as pious as the priest, but he is still expected to be a good example. Yet, the Levite in this story was equally as self-centered and perhaps just as prejudiced as the priest.

We are then introduced to the Samaritan. He's a Gentile, but we don't know if he is young or old, wealthy or poor. However, according to the text, the Samaritan's generosity was costly. To bring yesterday into today, on a $45k annual salary, that equates to one denarius at $173. The Samaritan gave the innkeeper two denarii ($346) after one night, with a promise to return and give him more.

Finally, there's the innkeeper. We don't know if he knows the Samaritan or not. He doesn't know how long the Samaritan will be gone. There is no guarantee he's actually coming back. Who knows how long it will take for this guy to recover, and can the stranger who dropped him off afford to pay me? In a week, that bill is over $2k. That's over $100k/year. Remember, in this hypothetical situation, you only make around $45k. Houston, we have a problem, and the only solution to this problem is love.

This whole story illustrates what love should and should not do. Love should have kept the robbers from robbing this man. Love should've caused the priest and the Levite to take care of him. Love stopped the Samaritan, and with all things unknown, I would argue that love made the innkeeper keep the stranger despite the possibility that he would not ever see the Samaritan again.

Maybe it was his love for money, or maybe it was his benevolence towards humanity. Who are we to judge his motive? Here's what I know: if it looks like love, sounds like love, and most importantly, acts like love, I'm calling it love. And this love, this desire to see others do well, be well, and stay well, this love for one's neighbor that meets needs, this love that is not by accident but a conscientious choice, this love is the kind of love that Jesus is calling for when he says, "Go and do likewise."

Jesus is not asking us to do to be loved. He is clarifying the fact that we love, therefore we do. Love is a motivator for action. Boyd Bailey argues that love reigns supreme because it brings out the best of both the lover and the loved, acting as a visible force that protects and compels us to give of ourselves while generating goodwill and trust.[18]

No matter which of the six we identify with, this is the love we are all called to by Christ. So, what will you do likewise this week? How will you show love to your neighbor? Be it a friend, family, or stranger? How will you answer the call to be benevolent?

I urge you to stop looking the other way when you have the means to help. Instead, it means helping whenever you encounter someone who could use your assistance. And that's when you'll find that those who are happiest are those who do the most for others. Let's be clear, Jesus doesn't teach us to empty our wallets for those who can and

---

[18] Boyd Bailey, *Two Minutes in the Bible for Men: A 90-Day Devotional* (Harvest House Publishers, 2016).

should be caring for themselves and their own families. Don't get taken advantage of. What Jesus is teaching us is to help people who genuinely cannot help themselves. Sometimes helping others is not about a handout but a hand up.

Who Is My Neighbor?

I cannot let this powerful lesson go by without addressing the elephant in the room. As we wrestle with Jesus's parable, we must speak on the fact that, as far as I can tell, throughout the history of mankind, there has always been the problem of racism. Of course, human history has always struggled with other sins such as sexism, classism, terrorism, and even individualism, but none of these other isms have been as destructive and stubborn as racism.

Racism is the Goliath that refuses to die — the titan that breeds like roaches. It is the false god that has been worshiped for centuries by people who either fear the success of others or blame others for their own lack of success. Racism is built upon and maintained by a lie that we are not the same.

I have, in my short lifetime, found in every race those who are rich as well as poor, those who are healthy, and those in need of medical care. I have discovered that race does not dictate one's ability to learn, nor does it determine one's ability to care for others. It is common among us all to live and die. I have met people of all ages, shapes, and sizes, from tall to short, introverted to extroverted, of every kind, whether their native tongue is English, Spanish, Afrikaans, or Tagalog. I assume you have too. You have met rude Americans, broke Americans, homeless Americans, thieving, murderous, adulterous, and scandalous Americans who look like you, talk like you, live where you live, and work where you work.

Perhaps our differences have less to do with race than we think. So why are our neighborhoods segregated? Why do our churches lack diversity, and why do we judge based on skin tone? I am a critic of those who suggest they don't see color, because when you choose to ignore color, you choose to deny the actual collective beauty that makes up humanity. It is our differences that make us a fantastic work of art. By God's design, we are not monochromatic. Its color, amongst other things, separates us from the zebra. But even zebras have different stripes. I choose to see color because in color I find different stories, perspectives, and backgrounds.

It is the contrast of color that makes the rose stand out, the rainbow worth looking at, and the skin shade worth admiring. Yet, we despise color because it separates. Its lines are distinct, and by nature, it dictates labels. We have judged, or at least know, people who have judged others not by their character but by their color. Racism is most apparent in this. It is a strange thing, but it is a familiar thing. As I mentioned earlier, racism is nothing new, but it still is strange. It's strange to see a church that encourages it. It's strange to meet Christians who justify it. And it's strange to see religious leaders ignore it. Primarily, when Jesus, by his very actions, taught against it.

Many of us miss this. We know he taught us to love our neighbors. We know he said to love one another just as he loved us. We just recapped the story of the Good Samaritan; we've heard what Jesus said, but we often miss what he actually did. However, when it comes to love, I believe the disciples initially overlooked two key aspects, and the church still overlooks those two things today. It's a good chance that if we catch it this time, the church can get back to the business of making disciples.

Let's go back to Adam and Eve, the young couple that had the responsibility of populating the earth. But before they reproduced, they brought sin into the world, and so, everything they reproduced came with a sin nature. This became evident in their eldest son, Cain, slaying his baby brother. Over time, things continued to deteriorate until the time of Noah. I guess you've heard the story. God spares Noah and his family but sends a flood that wipes out the rest of the planet in order to start again. The new batch, unfortunately, was just as bad, if not worse than the first.

In a moment, we will discuss the details of how an invasion by God led to a time of segregation, and then I'll tell you how His subsequent invasion led to desegregation. Still, after that comes yet another invasion that is currently simultaneously segregating and desegregating all the people on the earth. And that is where we will spend most of our time in this chapter. However, first, let's discuss the first two invasions, starting with the one that led to divine segregation.

Divine Segregation

Gen 11:1-9

In Genesis 11:1–9, Moses wrote:

> Now the whole world had one language and a common speech. As people moved eastward, they found a plain in Shinar and settled there. They said to each other, "Come, let's make bricks and bake them thoroughly." They used brick instead of stone, and tar for mortar. Then they said, "Come, let us build ourselves a city, with a tower that reaches to the heavens, so that we may make a name for ourselves; otherwise we will be scattered over the face of the whole earth." But the Lord came down to see the city and the tower the people were building. The Lord said, "If as one people speaking the same language they have begun to do this, then nothing they plan to do will be impossible for them. Come, let us go down and confuse their language so they will not understand each other." So the Lord scattered them from there over all the earth, and they stopped building the city. That is why it was called Babel—because there the Lord confused the

language of the whole world. From there the Lord scattered them over the face of the whole earth.

Moses then tells of the subsequent invasion that led to desegregation in Genesis 22:12–18. It reads as follows:

> "Do not lay a hand on the boy," he said. "Do not do anything to him. Now I know that you fear God, because you have not withheld from me your son, your only son." Abraham looked up and there in a thicket he saw a ram caught by its horns. He went over and took the ram and sacrificed it as a burnt offering instead of his son. So Abraham called that place The Lord Will Provide. And to this day it is said, "On the mountain of the Lord it will be provided." The angel of the Lord called to Abraham from heaven a second time and said, "I swear by myself, declares the Lord, that because you have done this and have not withheld your son, your only son, I will surely bless you and make your descendants as numerous as the stars in the sky and as the sand on the seashore. Your descendants will take possession of the cities of their enemies, and through your offspring all nations on earth will be blessed, because you have obeyed me."

I hope you were paying attention. If so, then you can see that this is where Jewish nationalism comes into play. For those who understand their heritage, they are not proud to be Jewish just for the sake of being Jewish. What makes them proud is the fact that they know who they are in God.

They know they have a promise from him. One that calls them blessed. Whether they are in the city or in the fields, coming or going, and even in tough times, they know that God never fails His children.

Christians today could learn much from this. Because of Biblical history, we know that God can do anything but fail. Our ancestors may not have had much, but along the way, they learned that God is more than enough. I grew up in a church that testified to God's goodness by reminding us that He is water when we're thirsty and bread when we're hungry. He's a lawyer in the courtroom and a doctor in the sick room. And the promises to his ancient children are theirs. But there's a promise for his children today, too.

This is the good news concerning Jesus the Christ. In fact, He is the fulfillment of this long-awaited promise. He is the blessing that will bless others, and he begins with the seed of Abraham, but thank God, he doesn't end there. He is the invasion that all the other invasions had been set up to bring. He is the ultimate extraterrestrial, the real Superman, the alien who brings life rather than takes it away.

He is God in the flesh. He is the manifestation of all that is good and Holy. He was there from the beginning, and he will be there in the end. Yet, he was sent to invade this earth to save those who couldn't save themselves. This invasion is different from the others. It is neither segregation nor desegregation.

I hope I still have your attention. This part is too important to rush, so let's take our time to think it through together. So far, we've seen how one invasion led to segregation when God interrupted the prideful plans of man. Then we saw how God invaded Abraham's space and called him to impact the nations. He was instructed to leave his father's house and his people and go to a place God would show him and give to him as an inheritance. It was a divine desegregation of sorts. Finally, the next few verses we're about to read reveal how the person of Jesus Christ became the invasion that led to desegregation.

Segregated Desegregation

In Matthew 15, we are invited to join Jesus as he preaches a passionate sermon to people who don't seem to like him much. It all started because, apparently, Jesus' disciples failed to wash their hands before eating. Matthew tells us that some Pharisees and teachers of the law came to Jesus from Jerusalem and asked, "Why do your disciples break the tradition of the elders? They don't wash their hands before they eat!" Jesus replied, "And why do you break the command of God for the sake of your tradition?"

Wow! That escalated quickly! Let's read on to find out why Jesus was so upset.

> Matthew 15:4–12 For God said, 'Honor your father and mother' and 'Anyone who curses their father or mother is to be put to death.' 5 But you say that if

anyone declares that what might have been used to help their father or mother is 'devoted to God,' 6 they are not to 'honor their father or mother' with it. Thus, you nullify the word of God for the sake of your tradition. 7 You hypocrites! Isaiah was right when he prophesied about you: 8 " 'These people honor me with their lips, but their hearts are far from me. 9 They worship me in vain; their teachings are merely human rules.'" 10 Jesus called the crowd to him and said, "Listen and understand. 11 What goes into someone's mouth does not defile them, but what comes out of their mouth, that is what defiles them." 12 Then the disciples came to him and asked, "Do you know that the Pharisees were offended when they heard this?"

It is impossible to have a strong opinion about anything without offending someone. As a pastor, sometimes I search hard for the words to use that will encourage you to see things God's way, in a way that won't hurt your feelings. But Jesus didn't work that hard. I'm trying to be more like Jesus, which means that sometimes you won't like what I have to say, but you probably need to hear it. Anyway, watch how Jesus responds after the disciples tell him that he hurt somebody's feelings.

Matthew 15:13–14 He replied, "Every plant that my heavenly Father has not planted will be pulled up by the roots. 14 Leave them; they are blind guides. If the blind lead the blind, both will fall into a pit."

Savage right? But it gets more intense. Keep reading.

Matthew 15:15–16 Peter said, "Explain the parable to us." 16 "Are you still so dull?" Jesus asked them.

Okay, so Jesus is clearly triggered. And they didn't have Snickers back then, but maybe after this, somebody started carrying around figs because hangry is real. Jesus explains:

> Matthew 15:17–20 "Don't you see that whatever enters the mouth goes into the stomach and then out of the body? 18 But the things that come out of a person's mouth come from the heart, and these defile them. 19 For out of the heart come evil thoughts—murder, adultery, sexual immorality, theft, false testimony, slander. 20 These are what defile a person; but eating with unwashed hands does not defile them."

Then Jesus abruptly ended the conversation and moved on to the region of Tyre and Sidon, where he met a Canaanite woman who desperately wanted Jesus to heal her demon-possessed daughter. Matthew's narrative is intense and in some ways, difficult to understand. Some might argue that what we are about to read seems uncharacteristic of the Jesus we learned about in Vacation Bible School.

> Matthew 15:21–24 Leaving that place, Jesus withdrew to the region of Tyre and Sidon. 22 A Canaanite woman from that vicinity came to him, crying out, "Lord, Son of David, have mercy on me!

> My daughter is demon-possessed and suffering terribly." 23 Jesus did not answer a word. So his disciples came to him and urged him, "Send her away, for she keeps crying out after us." 24 He answered, "I was sent only to the lost sheep of Israel."

Does Jesus's response bother you? It bothers me because I don't want to think of an angry Jesus. We struggle to understand a frustrated, irritated, or aggravated Jesus. But this is the exact Jesus Matthew reveals to us. A Jesus who was so triggered by the crowd that he ignored a woman in need. The disciples must have gathered that if Jesus didn't care, then they shouldn't either. But what I've learned since walking with Jesus is that sometimes, the richest lessons are in the moments when God is silent.

It's in silence, when God isn't speaking, that we have to ask ourselves what we know of His character. When God is silent, what am I supposed to do? How should I behave? I've been praying about my marriage, but God hasn't answered me. I have some decisions to make regarding my job, but God hasn't revealed to me which way to go. I'm desperate for a word, and God is with me, I know it. But still, he remains silent. Desperation cries out, and God is saying nothing. The pain in my life is like a screeching chalkboard, and Jesus doesn't even flinch. And when he finally speaks on the issue, He says something that we wouldn't expect him to say. He says, "I was sent only to the lost sheep of Israel."

What does that even mean? Well, she either didn't know, or didn't care, or both.

> Matthew 15:25–28 The woman came and knelt before him. "Lord, help me!" she said. 26 He replied, "It is not right to take the children's bread and toss it to the dogs." 27 "Yes it is, Lord," she said. "Even the dogs eat the crumbs that fall from their master's table." 28 Then Jesus said to her, "Woman, you have great faith! Your request is granted." And her daughter was healed at that moment.

When you're desperate enough, you don't care what other people think of you. When you're hurting, you don't care what they say about you. When you want God to do something in your life, you stop worrying about etiquette, rules, and tradition. And this kind of hunger is what Jesus responds to. He doesn't care if you are Jewish or French. He's not interested in your heritage or your birthright. God is looking for people who will look beyond the external and see Him as the God of all people.

It was her faith that bridged the gap when her race was a barricade. Jesus responded to this Canaanite woman as if she were the seed of Abraham because she treated him like he was just as much her God as He was theirs. It is only when we honor God that we prove who we are as sons and daughters, whether by birth or adoption. This woman made their God her God. And as far as the blessing is concerned, she decided in her heart that I may not deserve it, but I'm believing God for it. I don't need all the blessings, but I'll take the crumbs. And I don't care who likes me, I just need Jesus to like me. I just need God to see my faith. And here is what Jesus was teaching his disciples, and this is what God would say to us.

That is, I don't care what color they are; if they believe in me, that makes them my child. Just like I blessed you, I'll bless them. Just like I healed you, I'll heal them. And though I was sent to the lost sheep of Israel, the door is open to all who believe. If you read more of Matthew, you will find in the 11th chapter that Jesus calls out to those who recognize their need for Him.

Matthew 11:28–30 "Come to me, all you who are weary and burdened, and I will give you rest. 29 Take my yoke upon you and learn from me, for I am gentle and humble in heart, and you will find rest for your souls. 30 For my yoke is easy, and my burden is light."

I argue vehemently that it doesn't matter what color I am — whether black, white, yellow, or green — I can find rest in Jesus. And if Jesus is in you, then I should be able to find rest from the things in this world that divide and cause pain when I'm in the presence of His people. If we want to end racism, we should start loving God's children, no matter how different they are. Let me remind you again. Love meets needs, especially the needs of those who are crying out for help.

It's time for the miracle questions. What would our world look like if we stopped looking away from injustice and stood up for the oppressed? We wouldn't need signs that read "Stop Asian Hate" if we showed love to our Asian community in times of need. We wouldn't need to say "Black Lives Matter" if we treated them like they did. We wouldn't put all of our white brothers and sisters in the same boat as the evil men and women who did horrible things as individuals if we understood that the same God is father to us all. If we can't come to an agreement on anything else, let us allow our faith in God to build the bridge that unites us.

Galatians 3:26–29 So in Christ Jesus you are all children of God through faith, 27 for all of you who were baptized into Christ have clothed yourselves with Christ. 28 There is neither Jew nor Gentile, neither slave nor free, nor is there male and female, for you are all one in Christ Jesus. 29 If you belong to Christ, then you are Abraham's seed, and heirs according to the promise.

Now, we all know people who are living a life we'd love to live. Or maybe they have some things we'd like to have, and even need. But we also know people who are less fortunate than we are. You may be broke, but she's homeless. You might have haters, but folks are trying to murder him literally. You argued with your spouse last night, but the couple down the street just divorced after 20 years of marriage.

So yes, we would love for someone to meet our needs. But someone is praying that you would see, and meet theirs as well. And Love says, "If I can help, I will". I don't have to like you to love you. I don't have to like you to meet your need. I don't have to like you to save you from drowning, to feed you when you're hungry, or clothe you when you're naked. I don't have to like you, but if I'm going to call myself a Christian, a follower, or a disciple of Christ, well then, I have to love you, and as we all know, Love Meets Needs!

Loving the Hell Out of Them

Love is not only about what we do for others. It also includes what we do not do to them. In Matthew 18, Jesus explains why it's a bad idea to be the one responsible for someone else's falling away from the faith. In other words, Jesus is telling us not to be guilty of another person's church hurt. Church-hurt survivors are typically people who have experienced the pain of being treated poorly by other believers or church-goers.

Matthew 18 records Jesus's conversation where he said that it would be better for them to have a millstone tied around their neck and drown in the sea than to cause pain to those who believe in Him. The point of that passage was that offenses will come in any community, but we should work to be building blocks, and not stumbling blocks. Our job is to be repairers of the breach, or bridge builders who connect people to our Lord and Savior, Jesus the Christ. And that is something we cannot do as long as we put our desires, feelings, wants, and needs ahead of his. So, Jesus continues in Matthew 18:10, "See that you do not despise one of these little ones. For I tell you that their angels in heaven always see the face of my Father in heaven."

In other words, Christ instructs us to ensure that we are not guilty of harming or mistreating God's children. I think it's crucial that we understand that people don't stop being children of God just because we don't get along with them. Some of you may have multiple siblings, so you know that not everyone always gets along. Tension often accompanies close relationships, but it doesn't have to end them.

This is a big deal for several reasons. We have already learned that it would be better to drown than to make them stumble, but Jesus adds in this verse that God's children have angels in heaven who are assigned to them, and who, not sometimes, but always see the face of the Heavenly Father. That means they have intercessors who pray to God on their behalf about how you treat them.

Now, although God is omniscient, meaning he is all-knowing, and has an all-seeing eye, there is an element of advocacy added for those who have surrendered their lives to God. This is then a warning to the wicked and a comfort to the believer. If you are a child of God, you can rest assured that heaven is on your side! As we examine verse 12, we find a parable from Jesus that helps us understand this even further. That's one of the things I love about the gospels. There is so much depth and sometimes mysteries about Kingdom things, but Jesus often takes time to clear the fog.

Matthew 18:12 “What do you think? If a man owns a hundred sheep, and one of them wanders away, will he not leave the ninety-nine on the hills and go to look for the one that wandered off?”

> The Africa Bible Commentary expounds on this verse, and Adeyemo explains that “These little ones have direct access to his presence, and if they should be deceived by someone or something and wander away, the Father does not rest until they are safely returned to the fold. The leaving of the ninety-nine sheep is not to be understood as a reckless act of abandonment (18:12). In Jesus’ day, shepherds worked in groups, and the diligent shepherd would have left them in the care of others—with the communal herd.”[19]

Okay, we need to pause here to discuss the church. Is this not what we are supposed to do and be? It’s not just the pastor’s job to care for people. We are all responsible for the care of God’s sheep. This is especially true for those in leadership positions. It doesn’t matter if you are a pastor, elder, minister, deacon, greeter, worship leader, evangelist, or maintenance person. We are all responsible for God’s flock. We need to understand the depth of God's love for us. He loves us so much that he created a system to remind us of that fact. That system is the Church!

---

[19] Tokunboh Adeyemo, *Africa Bible Commentary* (WordAlive Publishers; Zondervan, 2006).

So, Jesus leaves the ninety-nine in care of the under-shepherds, and look what happens when he finds them.

Matthew 18:13 "And if he finds it, truly I tell you, he is happier about that one sheep than about the ninety-nine that did not wander off."

Now, this doesn't mean we are supposed to test God for attention. There is a thin line between craving attention and actually falling away. But there's something else that should be understood about this. The falling away is not about someone deciding to leave your church and attend another ministry. Leaving your church is not the same as leaving the faith. How and why a person leaves a ministry is also vital. If you leave a church because you are offended, you should address that offense with the offender as soon as possible. If you leave the faith because someone has seriously hurt you, that too should be communicated, because people often don't even know they hurt you.

But if you have left the faith, the shepherds and under shepherds should be working to bring you back to the father before it is everlasting too late. Our will should be the same as the Father's will. And we don't have to guess what that is.

Matthew 18:14 "In the same way your Father in heaven is not willing that any of these little ones should perish."

God does not want you or your fellow believers to experience eternal and absolute separation from his presence. This is what Jesus is trying to make clear for us. We are responsible for doing whatever is necessary to live in peace with one another. We should be encouragers, mentors, and coaches who do what we do in the spirit of love and concern. All that we do and say should be from a place of compassion, concern, and commitment to conforming to the image of the Son.

Let's Be Clear

It would be neglectful of me to try to convince you to be an example of love to believers if I were to leave out the biblical definition of love. So, let's take a moment and consider Paul's description in 1 Corinthians 13. He writes:

> Love is patient, love is kind. It does not envy, it does not boast, it is not proud. It does not dishonor others, it is not self-seeking, it is not easily angered, it keeps no record of wrongs. Love does not delight in evil but rejoices with the truth. It always protects, always trusts, always hopes, always perseveres. Love never fails.

Wow! Paul uses fifteen verbs to describe love. That should remind you of something you read earlier. You remember. The part that said, "Love is a choice made evident by action!" Garland seems to agree, noting, "Love is not conveyed by words; it has to be shown. It can be defined only by what it does and does not do".[20] Leon Morris provides brilliant commentary on 1 Corinthians 13, arguing, "Love reacts with goodness towards those who ill-treat it; it gives itself in kindness in the service of others".[21] Morris provides an explanation of every verb in the passage and humbly concludes,

> "The commentator cannot finish writing on this chapter without a sense that soiled and clumsy hands have touched a thing of exquisite beauty and holiness. Here, what is true of all Scripture is true in especial measure, that no comment can be adequate to so great a theme. Yet no commentator can excuse himself from the duty of trying to make plain what these matchless words have come to signify for him. And no Christian can excuse himself from the duty of trying to show in his life what these words have come to mean for him."[22]

I agree with Morris. So, after you read this chapter, consider these words with every person you encounter, and remind yourself to be benevolent. And if you're with someone who doesn't like their neighbor, don't enable them

---

[20] David E. Garland, *1 Corinthians*, Baker Exegetical Commentary on the New Testament (Grand Rapids, MI: Baker Academic, 2003), 616.

[21] Leon Morris, *1 Corinthians: An Introduction and Commentary*, vol. 7, Tyndale New Testament Commentaries (Downers Grove, IL: InterVarsity Press, 1985), 177.

[22] Leon Morris, *1 Corinthians: An Introduction and Commentary*, vol. 7, Tyndale New Testament Commentaries (Downers Grove, IL: InterVarsity Press, 1985), 183.

to act outside of love. Remind them also to be benevolent! Remember, love meets needs!

How Deep is Your Love

A few years ago, after my son graduated from high school, my wife and I took the kids on a family vacation to Cancun. We had a wonderful trip in the sun and did everything from ziplines to jungle tours on horseback and ATVs. Jen is a detailed planner, so she scheduled in everything from excursions to relax days at the resort, where we lounged by the pool, swam a little, and sunbathed on the beach.

My daughter is not a strong swimmer, but she did pretty well at the pool on our rest day, which gave us some confidence that she would be able to handle the next day's excursion that consisted of a trip to one of Mexico's finest sonatas. When the morning arrived, we boarded the van with other passengers and our tour guides for the Sonata, but upon arrival, we were a little surprised by the number of people present at the location. For context, this was near the peak of the COVID-19 pandemic, and many people were still hesitant to travel.

The large crowd was problematic, mainly because by the time we arrived, there were no life vests available for rent. Jen talked to my daughter about how well she had done in the pool, and since the water was clear, there was an additional element of safety provided for us if she felt like getting into the water. Additionally, there was a young couple from Italy with us, who claimed to be expert swimmers and promised to help if anything went wrong.

Well, things did go wrong, and when they did, the so-called experts did not help. My wife tells the story much better than I do. I will certainly leave out details, but the meat of the message is not lost. I will now do my best to tell it like she would.

There we were, enjoying the view of the jungle and taking in all of its glory. My wife stood on the edge of the sonata with my daughter and talked with her about how well she had been swimming in the pool at the resort. She pointed to the water and showed her how clear it was, and they agreed to jump into the water together.

Ideally, jumping in together would give my daughter, Nina, the extra boost of confidence, along with our new friends' promises to help her if she needed assistance. Nina agreed, and on a count of three, she and my wife plunged into the water. Jen came up first and immediately asked, "Where is Nina?" Less than a second later, Jen suddenly went back underwater. Nina pulled her under in an attempt to reach the surface.

She succeeded, but it was obvious that she was not in control and was in deep panic as she stood on Jen's shoulders. Able to fight her off, my wife resurfaced to catch air, and Nina started screaming, "Help me!" I began swimming in that direction, and, as calmly as she could, but with fear in her eyes, my wife said, “I need you to get her.” As she swam away, I held on to my daughter and told her that I needed her to relax as much as possible and go belly up. She was not in a mental space to listen, and as soon as she was close enough, she pressed on my shoulders to ensure she was above water, not realizing that she pushed me under.

I swam back up to the top, fighting her off of me the entire way. I caught my breath for a brief second but could not tread because Nina was in a complete panick. Under again, I went and fought my way up again. Nearly exhausted, I looked at my wife and read her lips as she shouted, “Throw her to me!” With all the energy I had left, I pushed away Nina’s arms and turned her away from me. I then grabbed her by the waist and threw her as high and far as I possibly could towards Jen. It was enough for them to connect one hand while Jen held on to the bank of the sonata with the other.

Nina was saved, but I was in trouble. Exhausted, I sank to the bottom like a rock and prayed that God would give me enough air and strength to make it back to the top so that I could float on my back until I had enough energy to swim again. God answered that prayer, and we all lived to swim another day. In fact, right after the incident, the tour guide gave Nina a life preserver that he had purchased from another tourist. She jumped right back into the water, but Jen could not bring herself to swim for the rest of the day.

I told you this story for the express purpose of illustrating the profound impact a parent's love can have on their child. No matter what happens, be it discipline, correction, or rebuke, Nina knows that both of her parents love her enough to give their very lives for hers if necessary. This is the kind of love Jesus has for us, except his love is even more powerful in that he gave his life for people who never met him, those who rejected him, and even those who crucified him.

Chapter 4: Gotta Have Faith

Don't let anyone look down on you because you are young, but set an example for the believers in speech, in conduct, in love, in faith and in purity.

This chapter is all about faith. According to the writer of Hebrews, "Faith is a substance of things hoped for, the evidence of things not seen." (NKJV). The NIV words it this way: "Now faith is confidence in what we hope for and assurance about what we do not see,"[23] while The Message Bible presents it as: "The fundamental fact of existence is that this trust in God, this faith, is the firm foundation under everything that makes life worth living. It's our handle on what we can't see. [24]

As you strive to become a better version of yourself, you will need to understand the distinction between biblical faith and emotional faith, or hope. Faith, or Biblical hope, is characterized by a confident expectation based on God's promises. It is characterized by a confident expectation based on God's promises. This biblical hope or biblical faith has to be an anchor for believers.

The churches I typically associate with favor a song that declares, "My Soul has been anchored in the Lord." That is what Biblical Faith does. It anchors us in the word of God

---

[23] Eugene H. Peterson, *The Message: The Bible in Contemporary Language* (Colorado Springs, CO: NavPress, 2005), Heb 11:1–2.

[24] *The New International Version* (Grand Rapids, MI: Zondervan, 2011), Heb 11:1.

and our relationship with God, so that we remain steadfast, no matter what happens in our lives. As the song says, "But if the storms don't cease and if the winds keep blowing, My Soul Is Anchored in The Lord. Many people think they don't have faith, or they might think they have faith in certain things. The truth is that we all showcase some level of faith every single day. We all have faith in something or somebody. We are designed to have faith in something. That's just how God wired us.

For example, if you prepared your dinner for tonight, or bought breakfast food from the grocery store this week, it was because you thought you or your family would be home at some point and would need to eat. When you went to work last week, you believed that your job would still require your presence every day. Therefore, you groomed, got dressed, got in your car or whatever mode of transportation you take, and drove to work.

Next time you attend a church service, pay attention to what people do when they enter the sanctuary and take their seats. Chances are, you will not see anyone check the bolts or the screws in the seat they sit in. You probably won't see anyone turning over the chair or pushing on the pad to make sure that the seat will hold them when they sit on it.

Why? Because they had faith that the chair was going to hold them up? Steuart Brisco says, "Faith is only as valid as its object. You could have tremendous faith in very thin ice and drown, you could have very little faith in very thick ice and be perfectly secure. Faith is only as good as its object."[25] Perhaps you've noticed that faith shares many similarities with love. Like love is a choice, so is faith. That does not mean we're walking in blind faith. After all, blind faith is not true faith. Blind faith, best put, is a gamble. You don't know if it will work out or not. In contrast, true faith is based on God's credibility and his promises.

Now would be a great time to take a moment to reflect on your life. Think about anything that's going on in your life right now, and before you decide to take action, ask yourself, "What does God's word say about my current situation? Does God's word speak healing in my body? Is there a word for my disease? Is there a word for my finances? Is there a word for my marriage or my relationships? Does God have a word about raising children? is there a word for how I handle people who get on my nerves?

If you are a believer who can find a word, and especially if it's a word that is a promise from God concerning your life and my human experience, you can put faith in it. Everyone has something going on in life. There's got to be a word for it. There's a word for when I'm feeling depressed and down and out—a word that says there's peace that surpasses all understanding. There's a word that says God would give me perfect peace if I kept my mind on him!

It's reassuring to know that true faith is based on God's credibility and his promises. Consider the creation of the universe. Someone reading this book may have placed a great deal of faith in Darwinism. You totally believe in the

---

[25] Roy B. Zuck, *The Speaker's Qote Book*, Logos Research Edition (Kregel, 2004).

Big Bang Theory. You believe that all that is created is the result of a cosmic collision of random material. But when you think about the intricacies of the human body, how the brain works, how the heart works, how everything works together, and how just being just a tad bit off changes everything. When you consider how one chromosome can change everything in your life, thinking that something random could create something so beautiful takes a lot of faith.

On the other hand, those who have faith in what Moses taught about creation know that it is an intelligent design. Darwin wasn't there when the world was created, nor was Moses. I think about Moses and how he wrote his autobiography throughout the Pentateuch. Moses discusses his weaknesses – specifically, his lack of eloquence in speech and his tendency to become frustrated with people and impatient with God.

When you read his story, you know that he's just a man and that there's nothing about him that would make a pharaoh obey his command to let his, or rather, God's people go. When you think about Moses, it doesn't take long to conclude that Moses was not a perfect man. Moses had issues. He even murdered a guy. Yet, Moses, in all of his imperfections, admits, "You know, I wasn't there at the beginning, but God revealed to me how the beginning came to be."

Now, some people will argue for an Earth that is 8 billion years old. They look at the mountains and talk about carbon dating, which doesn't make logical sense to me because, still, you've got nothing from 8 billion years ago as a true point of reference. But you look at a mountain and you say there's no way that mountain is only a couple of thousand years old.

According to Moses, God reached down into the dust of the earth and created humanity with His hands, breathing the breath of life into them. Do you think that Adam was created as a baby? When God created Adam, He created him complete. He didn't say, "Baby, I created them male and female." He said, "Man I created, male and female." Thus, when he created Adam, Adam already knew how to walk. Adam didn't have to survive on breast milk because he had already developed everything he needed to eat like a mature human. He had teeth and strength in his jaws. He had the awareness to chew and swallow. Adam was so well-developed that when God created Adam, the first thing that God told Adam to do was to get to work.

Imagine Adam, created in his prime physical form with the ability to do everything that God had designed a man to do. Let's imagine that Adam was created with a 30-year-old body. Okay, to some, that's too old. Imagine a 25-year-old body. The point is that he's in his prime. He's emotionally intelligent, mentally aware, and he's strong, he's capable and ready to do what God has created him to do. Why? Because God designed him like that. Now, if God can design a man with all that it takes to be human, can he not do the same thing for a mountain?

To make a mountain look like a mountain is older than it actually is? Adam, in one day, looked 25. Can God not create a mountain and make it look 8 billion years old? These two belief systems require us to have faith in an event that no human has ever witnessed. You have to put your faith in something. The Christian view requires faith in God's word.

Let's explore Hebrews chapter 11. This chapter is often referred to as the Hall of Faith. It's called that because it lists a long list of people who please God by their faith. In verse 6, we are told that "we must have faith in order to please the Lord." It is impossible to please God without faith. I encourage you to read the entire chapter and study the details of each named person at your convenience. In the meantime, I want to highlight a few names that are familiar to most of us. The first one you all might remember is the man named Noah. Noah's faith was exemplified in his construction of the Ark. Despite public ridicule, the world had never seen rain before, but Noah built an ark to prepare for a flood that would come.

As a pastor, I have been blessed to lead a multi-generational church. God has entrusted us to minister to people from diverse backgrounds, with various persuasions, including those who grew up Lutheran, Catholic, Baptist, Pentecostal, Apostolic, and many more. God has given us the grace to minister effectively to people, even those with political differences. In this climate, it's tough to see families turning against each other because they disagree on their politics and violently separate over their preferred politician. For me, there are issues on both sides of the political spectrum that I agree with, and then there are aspects on both sides that I disagree with. However, none of those issues is powerful enough to make me dislike you.

I am greatly disappointed in the American people, but even more so, I'm ashamed of those who claim to be Christian. Part of me is sad because this happened before in my lifetime, and it's happening again in less than 10 years. Some people claim to be friends of mine on social media, including those I've known for a long time, as well as some I've just met, who are praying for the downfall of the government. Not on a political level, but on a local, everyday level, employees work hard to support and serve the people. So-called Christians are praying that all government employees lose their jobs.

I can't believe how they cheer knowing that their bi-vocational pastors, or close relatives and friends, are government employees. I do not currently receive a salary from the church I am graced to serve. I publicly asked those who are hoping that my wife and I lose our jobs, where they would attend church if we had to relocate to find work elsewhere and close the church doors here. Nevertheless, we have faith in God that our needs will be met, no matter the outcome.

I want to emphasize that faith is not merely a belief in God's existence. Christian faith involves trusting in God's faithfulness and acting accordingly. That means that what we believe, we act on. I receive phone calls, emails, and text messages every day from colleagues seeking answers to what is happening in our world. Recently, the thought hit me. There's a part of me that never really dug into the idea that

God uses some of us to be Ezras at our jobs. God is in need of Nehemias and Daniels. God, in His divine wisdom, has appointed some people to serve in government offices to make a difference in the government, just as He did with Daniel and the three Hebrew boys, and Ezra and Nehemiah, who rebuilt the city and the temple walls around Israel.

When we believe that our life is in God's hands, then we govern ourselves as if it is. I could be on this job and be like, "Man, I'm sick of this. I'm just gonna quit!" But there's a difference being made in somebody's life. There have been moments when I am at work after hours, trying to help someone with a work-related task, and in the midst of doing that work, God has opened doors of opportunity where I got to share some of the Gospel with people. Those are the moments that bring me joy as I think, if nothing else, this could be a big deal if this person retires in the next couple of days, and this could have been my only chance to share the gospel of Jesus Christ.

Getting back to the hall of faith, notice how Noah pleased the Lord. Consider how Abraham characterized his obedience to God by leaving his homeland and notice his willingness to sacrifice Isaac, which means that he either trusted God that God would either perform a miracle before he murdered his son, or that God would resurrect him.

Ladies, you're not excluded because Abraham's wife, Sarah, exemplified her faith. Sarah's faith is notable because she believed in God's promise that He would give her a descendant, despite her advanced age. Let's go with plain language. You see, she was old. She was well beyond childbearing years. We can say she was about 40 years or more beyond childbearing age, and she still had the deed done with the expectation that it would bear fruit.

If that's not faith, then I don't know what is. She probably had a bad back. Her hips probably hurt, but she performed because she believed! Are you still with me? It's not like she's had a baby before, so it's unlikely she calculated that this time it would produce a child. She'd been doing that. I need you to see that faith is not about knowledge of past experiences. Knowledge, at times, can be painful. Knowledge, at times, can make one miserable. In Ecclesiastes 1:18 we are told that with much wisdom comes much sorrow. The more knowledge, the more grief."

Ecclesiastes 12:11-12 says, "The words of the wise are like goads, their collected sayings like firmly embedded nails—given by one shepherd. Be warned, my son, of anything in addition to them. Of making many books there is no end, and much study wearies the body."

This proverb is most felt by those who have been to school. You know how much studying makes you feel. Have you ever been exhausted and told yourself, "I can't read another page right now. I'm tired and I don't even want to go hang out." In 1961, James Baldwin was asked a question by a radio host about being black in America. He said, "To be a negro in this country and to be relatively conscious is to be in a state of rage almost; almost all of the time, and in one's work and part of the rage is this. It isn't only what is happening to you, but it's what's happening all around, you and all of the time..." I repeat, faith isn't about what you know. Faith is about who you know. Knowing God makes all the difference in the decisions that you make, especially in tough times.

In 2025, the new administration attempted to remove Black History Month. In protest to this decision and as a display of resilience, I started posting a book by a black author on my social media every day because if our society doesn't want to acknowledge what we, as a people, have brought to the table, then we should. The reality is that no one can take black history from us. In fact, we are making black history. Faith isn't about what you know. It's about who you know.

I believe this is why Dr. Martin Luther King Jr., knowing that his life was threatened and knowing that his family could be targeted, still marched and fought against the evils of segregation and racism. He believed that it was God's will that we didn't have to experience what his parents and even what he had to endure. He believed that God had a word for the oppressed and disinherited. That's why he often quoted Moses and referenced the Exodus. It is why they sang those songs about freedom. It's why they marched for desegregation. As I look at the political and social climate in America, I fear that we're going to forget all of that horrible history and repeat those crucial mistakes.

Therefore, faith, if it is biblical, must include persuasion and conviction. You have to be persuaded, and you have to have a conviction in your heart that leads to corresponding action. This holds true, even for the most challenging aspects of life. If you're persuaded that it must be done and you have conviction in your heart, even though it's scary to do, you will have corresponding action. That means that you're operating in faith.

The better you is the byproduct of growing your faith. The question remains, then, how do I increase my faith? Romans 10:17 says, “faith comes from hearing the message and the message is heard through the word about Christ.” That is why Church attendance is important. We need to be hearing the word. I recommend being selective about what church you attend and what pastor you listen to. You need to guard what word you're submitting yourself to. Some people are frequently online, listening to word from whose lifestyles you don't even know. You have no idea if they're applying that word to their life. Does it work for them? You see them on TV and think that because they have a big church or following, they must be right. Yet, there's so much falsehood that comes over pulpits and across social media. Many are eating it up, and you don't know the spirit behind that word.

We’ve all witnessed celebrities get married, and a year later, they're giving marital advice. We don't know what their marriage is like. Do they argue over petty things? Do they hug and kiss in private like they do when the cameras are pointed at them? We know nothing about them, but a year later, after they have sold a million books, they're divorced. Ironically, those who purchased those books won’t even take sound marital advice from their pastor who has been married 25 years or more.

Young ministers often don't know what the online pastor’s church is really like, but they cling to a lot of information that is often not even biblical. But we love the aesthetics. They feature a large stage and a big crowd. They might have a couple of brothers in the pulpit cheering them on. Others subscribe to certain women with Jezebel spirits on because they love their YouTube channel. And since she has an itinerary full of preaching engagements, we assume she is faithful to God's word. But we are doubting everything we hear at our own churches on Sunday mornings.

These are the reasons why my wife and I try to be open books. We want people we disciple to see that we're living what we teach. How will we teach you how to manage your money if we are not disciplined with our money? How can I instruct a man to love his wife if my wife loathes me? Perhaps I'm on your toes, so let's move to 2 Timothy 2:15. Here's what Paul says. "Do your best..." Let's pause and reflect on those first three words. We need to adopt that mindset because we sometimes approach the things of God with a lack of enthusiasm. Dare I say that most times we approach God, and the work He invites us to partake in, like it's a hobby? We have a volunteer mentality. This contradicts the apostle Paul, who wrote that he is a servant of Christ. Do you know what that means? It means I don't have a choice in this.

Yet, we choose to stay in bed because it's more comfortable. We prefer not to get involved because it would be too much work. We decided to change churches simply because we didn't like being corrected. But Paul says I'm a servant. He intentionally uses slave language, and that offends us. He uses slave language to convey the fact that he has been bought with a price, and he wants us to understand that our lives belong to God.

When you understand that, your language will change. Like Paul, you will say, "I don't have a choice. When God says go, I have to go. When God says stay, I have to stay. When God says get out of bed, I must get out because I am a servant, and he's my master.

So, Paul says to Timothy, "Do your best." In other words, please don't be lazy about it. Don't be half-hearted about it. Please don't say you will do something and then don't do it. Don't say you will be there and then not show up. Do your best to present yourself to God – not to your pastor, the deacons, or social media. Do your best to present yourself to God as one who is approved as a worker, not one who needs to be ashamed.

Here is my question: The things that you're doing for the kingdom, assuming that you're doing something for the kingdom of God; if you were to present that gift to God, would you be ashamed of it? To say, God, I never studied, but I tried to teach from time to time. I sang on the worship team, but I never practiced the songs before I got to rehearsal. Are you doing your best to show yourself approved?

Dear preacher, teacher, or evangelist, God has entrusted us with His Word, and there are ways to handle it that are not always right. We can mishandle God's word to get the applause of men. I see it all the time. Some of these social media ministries really irk me because some people take the word, manipulate it, and use it for likes. People build their entire platform by gossiping about other preachers and pastors. I don't understand how anyone has time to be a pastor and focus so much on how some other Pastor is so wrong. Some preachers spend more time preaching about other preachers than they do about Jesus. I don't understand it. Who has time for that?

I digress. However, we're accountable for how we handle the word of truth. In short, don't be just hearers of God's word. Handle it during your work week. Handle it at school or in your marriage. Handle it in your relationships. Handle it with care. It is dangerous to treat the word of Truth and God's commands as suggestions. That's mishandling the word of Truth.

Hebrews 5:11-4 We have much to say about this, but it is hard to make it clear to you because you no longer try to understand.

He's saying, "You're not even trying to understand! You won't read. You refuse to study. You won't even take the time to watch a video. The author is upset because his audience refuses to take any steps that will help them grow. They don't work at it. They ignore opportunities for it. You're not even trying. Pastors understand the anguish of it all. Teaching those who need it most but refuse to listen gets exhausting. Ministry leaders and Bible teachers worldwide are lamenting, "I have so much that I want to share with you, but you won't even try to hear what God is saying to the church." The writer adds, "though by this time you ought to be teachers, but you need someone to teach you the elementary truths of God's word."

We are going over the basics of the faith all over again. We've been down this road. We have discussed this extensively before. How are we still here? How are we still talking about adultery as if we do not know it's wrong? How are we still talking about fornication like we don't know the dangers of loose lifestyles? How are we still talking about drunkenness like we are clueless about how it damages the body, mind, and relationships? Why do we still have to argue over that? How are we still unable to talk to you plainly about the righteousness of God and what it means to be a champion of the faith? I would love to discuss deeper topics with you, but we are still focused on basic principles, such as loving your neighbor.

In Hebrews 5:12-13 he writes, "You need someone to teach you the elementary truths all over again. You need, milk not solid food. Anyone who lives on milk being still an infant is not acquainted with the teachings about righteousness." This is why you struggle to give generously. You don't even have salvation down yet. You don't even know what it means to be saved. Of course, I can't teach you about stewardship. You don't know what it means to be a minister or a deacon. The words "minister" and "deacon" mean the same thing. They both mean servant. I can't even talk to you about that because you're not even saved.

There is wickedness in high places. We are wrestling against spiritual things, and you want to argue over Acts 2:38 against Matthew 28:18-20? Therefore, we are stuck on these basic things because many people are not even trying to understand the deeper aspects of faith. I think the writer of Hebrews is quite upset. Let's read the next line.

Heb 5:13-14 …being still an infant, you're not acquainted with the teachings about righteousness. But solid food is for the mature…

Understand, mature people can be corrected without being offended. They know that just because someone invited you to an argument doesn't mean you have to attend. Mature people understand what Jesus meant when he said, "Love those who hate you and pray for those who falsely accuse you." Mature people get that. They know to guard their gates. They realize that you can't listen to every conversation or watch everything on TV and the internet.

Mature people know that you can't eat junk food all week long and expect to be healthy at the end of the week. That's why some folks come to church and can't even get involved in the worship service. If you've been engulfed in mess all week long, you will struggle to sense God's presence. Let me encourage you to limit the amount of attention you give to social media. Jesus said that in the last days, many false prophets would rise up and people would have itching ears. That means that you'll be going wherever you can to hear only words that you already agree with. It doesn't matter if that word is truth or not. As long as it makes you feel good, you are happy with it.

So, you want someone to scratch your ear and make you feel good about what they have to say, instead of allowing God's words to motivate you to become the best version of yourself.

Heb 5:14 Solid food is for the mature who by constant use have trained themselves have trained themselves to distinguish good from evil.

You distinguish good from evil by knowing the word of God. Personally, when I'm studying to teach, I typically don't look at what commentators have to say until I have wrestled with what I believe God is saying through the passage. Then I read commentaries. If there's a commentator who argues the opposite of what I noticed, I wrestle with the text a little more to discover the truth. If I conclude that my initial perspective was incorrect, I will revise my argument before presenting it. If I'm right, I'll bless God for the insight.

Dear young preachers and teachers, you must wrestle with the text and prove yourself worthy to carry God's word. The only way to do that is to immerse yourself in God's Word. You cannot only hear or read God's word when you attend Sunday morning worship services. That will stunt your spiritual growth. Be an example to the believer in speech, in Life or conduct, in love, and in faith. You cannot please God without faith, and you cannot have faith without knowing God's word. Please make it a habit to start reading and meditating on God's Word daily.

King David said in Psalm 119:11, Thy word have I hidden in my heart that I might not sin against thee.

Do you know why that's important? It is important because what's in your heart when it's squeezed comes out. If cursing is in your heart when pressure hits, cussing comes out, but if the word of God is in your heart when you step your toe, you say Jesus instead of those other words. And

Jesus says it's not what is in you that what goes in you that defiles a man. It's what comes out of you when you're under pressure. Is it God's word or the devil's?

I'd love for you to join me in a short prayer as we conclude this chapter. I hope you will pray this out loud: Father, we thank you for this understanding. We thank you for speaking to us. We thank you for allowing us to hear your word once again so that we can act on your word and help us not just be hearers but doers. God, help us increase our faith through our knowledge of Your Word. We thank you for it in Jesus' name, amen.

Chapter 5: Purity

As we prepare to explore the final characteristic Paul instructs Timothy to exemplify, I would like to address the issue of biblical literacy in America. Studies show that the majority of Americans who claim to be Christian do not read the Bible regularly. Fewer people memorize scripture, and some who do often misquote. I argue that this is why people often struggle to know how to act or respond Christianly in the face of external stimuli. This is troubling because whatever is in us will come out when we face challenging situations.

For example, instead of scripture coming out of our mouths, Rap or Rock lyrics come out in stressful moments. Some might even sing sad Country songs in a given situation whose lyrics contradict God's Word. Why? Because that is what's in you, and what's in you is what comes out of you. In this chapter, I invite you to challenge yourself to be more faithful in your personal Bible study for the simple reason that it is impossible to get closer to God through His word without being changed in the process. This change requires an emptying of ourselves. That is what I understand Paul to mean by purity in 1 Timothy 4:12. I'll explain.

In the Old Testament, the basic sense of the Hebrew word for purity is probably an emptying out or a state of being clean. The verb appears about 40 times, most of them with an ethical, moral, or forensic sense. For example, in Numbers 5, the Israelites are commanded to "send away" those considered unclean. They were to "empty out" the camp in order to make it pure. Proverb 20:9 reads, "Who can say, 'I have kept my heart pure; I am clean and without sin"?[26] Finally, in Ezekiel 36:26-27, we understand purification not just as emptying out, but as replacement. It reads, "I will give you a new heart and put a new spirit in you; I will remove from you your heart of stone and give you a heart of flesh. And I will put my Spirit in you and move you to follow my decrees and be careful to keep my laws".[27]

Externally, purity includes being free of ritual contamination. In Old Testament times, people contracted ritual impurity by coming into contact with a corpse and certain dead animals. They were also considered impure due to the involuntary flow of fluids from the sexual organs, certain diseases, or the eating of prohibited foods. Finally, particular objects were regarded as pure while others were thought of as impure.

Crossing the bridge into modern application, Paul wants us to understand that while it is important to empty ourselves for God's Holy Spirit to fill us up, there must also be a habit of abstaining from external situations and sometimes, people who may corrupt that which is meant to be set apart for God's use. This argument is more clearly made in Romans 12:1-2, where Paul writes, "Therefore, I urge you, brothers and sisters, in view of God's mercy, to

---

[26] *The New International Version* (Grand Rapids, MI: Zondervan, 2011), Pr 20:9.

[27] *The New International Version* (Grand Rapids, MI: Zondervan, 2011), Eze 36:26–27.

offer your bodies as a living sacrifice, holy and pleasing to God—this is your true and proper worship. Do not conform to the pattern of this world, but be transformed by the renewing of your mind. Then you will be able to test and approve what God's will is—his good, pleasing and perfect will".

When Paul refers to your bodies as a living sacrifice, he means to direct his readers to the altar in the temple used for offerings. Such sacrifices were expected to meet God's standards. They should be ceremonially clean and used for no other purpose outside of what God intended them for. Thus, the term "holy" fundamentally means to be set apart for a specific use. Paul is calling his readers to be sanctified, or dedicated to divine service. This requires a sending away, an emptying of all that is impure. It is an explicit call for purity.

I'm intentionally slow-walking this idea because purity is the final ingredient in Paul's exemplary cake called Christianity. Having all other characteristics or ingredients, but without the icing, makes a cake nothing more than sweet bread. The icing completes the cake. It's what makes it beautiful and appealing to the one to whom the cake is meant to honor.

My wife and daughter love watching baking shows in which competitors are judged on their cake-decorating skills. While they are judged on the cake's texture and flavors, I've noticed that some contestants get away with undercooked cakes because they do such a great job with the aesthetics. Undoubtedly, you have been to parties or other social events and have seen extravagant-looking cakes, but have found their taste or texture disappointing. The icing, the décor, everything that enhances the cake's appearance makes room for grace.

That's what purity does. It adds a layer of grace whereby people can say, "I know he said the wrong thing, but his motive was pure. He didn't mean it like he said it." Purity allows one to err in conduct, and your friends or family will give you the benefit of the doubt because your heart was in the right place. When they fail to speak your love language, purity makes up for that. Purity makes room for grace when the young preacher misinterprets scripture during a sermon. This is the example Paul encourages Timothy to set.

R.C. Sproul correctly argues, "Purity is not excluded from the idea of the holy; it is contained within it. But the point we must remember is that the idea of the holy is never exhausted by the idea of purity. It includes purity, but is much more than that. It is purity and transcendence. It is a transcendent purity."[28] Indeed, purity is not the end-all, be-all, but it is a characteristic that all who are should strive to exemplify.

---

[28] R. C. Sproul, *The Holiness of God*, LOGOS (Tyndale House Publishers, 1993).

Thanks Dad

As I write this chapter, my father is in an intensive care unit (ICU) in Nashville, TN. He is in a medically induced coma and is on a ventilator. Because of an acute kidney condition, he needs dialysis. He is being treated for five types of infection and pneumonia. The medical team is working hard to purge his system of all impurities. If you were to see him in this state, it would be hard to believe that just a week ago, he bathed and dressed himself in a tuxedo and attended a gala as one of the hosts of our annual conference, The National Gathering of Champions. But if he is to survive this, it will be by the grace of God and the wisdom of the doctors and nurses who helped him to detox his body.

Moments like these cause us to reminisce and reflect on our time spent with our loved ones. One of the things I most admire about my dad is that he hardly ever says anything negative about people or situations. Those who know him can tell that he hates gossip and lives by the rule that if you don't have anything nice or uplifting to say, do not say anything at all. He will kill a gossip session by saying something positive about the person you are talking about. He will show grace by suggesting reasons for their unbecoming behavior. My dad hated toxic speech and behavior, and he refused to tolerate it from us.

My siblings would tell you that we were not allowed to call each other stupid in his presence. We were not permitted to tell our siblings to "shut up" either. Even in adulthood, if my siblings are not getting along, my father reminds us to love each other because they are the only siblings we have. We used to laugh about that because my parents had five of us. Nevertheless, he is right. Life is too short to be at odds with others. Dad taught us to forgive quickly. Forgiveness is a detox.

In Philippians 4, the Apostle Paul writes to the church in Philippi, encouraging them to rejoice in the Lord always and to live in harmony with one another. Personally, this is one of my favorite chapters in scripture because it serves as a constant reminder to believers, what the church community should look like. Concerning this chapter, Stubs correctly observes, "He grounds the exhortation for communal unity in the now-familiar concept of 'like-mindedness."[29] As I reflect on the wording of verses 8-9, I believe this is what my father has been trying to teach his children our entire lives, and what I now take responsibility for teaching not only my natural children but also those I now pastor. Let's review those words together.

> **Philippians 4:8-9 Finally, brothers and sisters, whatever is true, whatever is noble, whatever is right, whatever is pure, whatever is lovely, whatever is admirable—if anything is excellent or**

---

[29] Monya A. Stubbs, "Philippians," in *True to Our Native Land: An African American New Testament Commentary*, ed. Brian K. Blount et al. (Minneapolis, MN: Fortress Press, 2007), 374.

praiseworthy—think about such things. Whatever you have learned or received or heard from me, or seen in me—put it into practice. And the God of peace will be with you. [30]

Paul is administering the anti-virus to spiritual toxicity. He is giving us the prescription for the infection called sin. The bacteria causing pain, discomfort, fever, and illness in the body must be pushed out or emptied out through a hostile takeover. The truth is hostile to a lie. Nobility is an attack on indecency. Right is diametrical to wrong, and whatever is pure cannot occupy the same space as those things that are impure.

Paul continues to encourage his reader to think bout the things that re praiseworthy because praise kills gossip. Admiration shuts the mouths of haters, and as we all know, love covers a multitude of sin. But we cannot simply preach these things. We must live it. We have to become it through practice until we have perfected it. This is why Paul can say with confidence, "Be like me!" The Africa Bible Commentary argues, "Before accusing Paul of pride, it is worth remembering that before the New Testament books were written and accepted, the only standard for Christian teaching and behaviour was to be found in people who

---

[30] *The New International Version* (Grand Rapids, MI: Zondervan, 2011), Php 4:8–9.

accurately reflected the authority and ethical standards of our Lord".[31]

So, thanks, Dad, for teaching this principle to your children. Thank you for not simply telling us to think on these things, but for also showing us what it looks like to keep quiet when we cannot find anything good to say. Thank you for putting into practice the discipline of spiritual detox. You have set a great example of purity for all to see, and you are loved and appreciated for that. May my mouth be emptied of gossip. May my thoughts be optimistic in every situation.

Final Thoughts

When I began writing this chapter, my father was in the intensive care unit (ICU). He passed away two days before Christmas and merely days before I submitted my final draft. On the day of his funeral, I shared these words that testify to the man he was.

> Today I buried my father who was the best man I have ever known. He wasn't an athlete or musician. He was not a world-renowned preacher. He wasn't famous and he wasn't rich. He was a man who loved God and he loved people.

---

[31] Tokunboh Adeyemo, *Africa Bible Commentary* (Nairobi, Kenya; Grand Rapids, MI: WordAlive Publishers; Zondervan, 2006), 1473.

My father impacted so many people in so many ways, and I'm proud to be his son. But he is here no longer. Although he is resting in a much better place, I realize that for me and others who loved him, his departure is a felt loss. What this means for us is that while it is natural and completely human to mourn, we who are in Christ have the supernatural ability to celebrate not only his legacy, but his future.

But even in that, we give ourselves permission to wrestle with our temporal realities. That is, we know that weeping may endure for a night and joy comes in the morning, but we also know that for the rest of our lives, things will never be the same. We know to live is Christ and to die is gain, but we also know that we will no longer receive those phone calls with Papoo who is just making sure we're okay.

November 2025 was the last time I'll walk into his house and yell out, "Dadday!" as was my custom whenever I wanted to spend some time with him. So, I will need to establish new norms, new routines, and new traditions if I'm going to, not only survive without him, but continue to live in a way that would make my daddy proud. So, here's what I plan to do to manage loss.

I plan to take as much time off as I need so that I can properly mourn and begin the healing process. This means spending intimate time with God through prayer and meditating on his word. It also means spending time with people who I know are praying for me and genuinely love me. People like my wife and kids, my mentors and pastors, and my closest friends.

As I was preparing for this day, I was reminded of Jesus and how he mourned his cousin's death. Scripture reveals that Jesus took some time to get away, and upon his return, he began ministering to others' needs. This made me think of how He prayed for Simon in Luke 22:32, knowing that he was going to endure a dark season in life, Jesus said, "But I have prayed for you, Simon, that your faith may not fail. And when you have turned back, strengthen your brothers.""

And finally, I plan to set some new goals. For me, that includes writing and publishing more books, purchasing more property, and mentoring people who are serious about Kingdom business.

I hope to be an example to you and others for what it looks like to grieve as a believer. I know I'm not perfect, and someone might not agree with it. But that doesn't matter. No one can tell you or me how long to grieve, how to express your grief, or how to feel about your loss. But what I know is that God is watching, he knows my pain, and I pray that my way of handling this season brings glory to His name. For it is in him that I live, I move, and have my very being.

I find it best to conclude this chapter with one more verse from the sacred text. This one is an acrostic from the twenty-two letters of the Hebrew alphabet. While it is the longest psalm in scripture, the author is unknown. We won't recite it all, but I would be negligent in my duty as a teacher of God's word for leaving this out.

> **Psalm 119:9 How can a young person stay on the path of purity? By living according to your word. I seek you with all my heart; do not let me stray from your commands. I have hidden your word in my heart that I might not sin against you. Praise be to you, Lord; teach me your decrees. With my lips I recount all the laws that come from your mouth. I rejoice in following your statutes as one rejoices in great riches. I meditate on your precepts and consider your ways. I delight in your decrees; I will not neglect your word.**[32]

---

[32] *The New International Version* (Grand Rapids, MI: Zondervan, 2011), Ps 119:9–16.

Conclusion

In Chapter One, we discussed the importance of speech. We said that death and life are in the power of the tongue, and as the writer of Proverbs suggests, those who love it will eat the fruit thereof. That means if you love to speak unfruitful things, you're going to eat the fruit of death. Similarly, if you speak life, you're going to eat the fruits of life.

In Chapter Two, we addressed character, and when we discuss conduct, we cannot overlook that our reputation is intertwined with it. It's about integrity. Integrity is one of the Air Force's core values. In fact, it's the leading core value: Integrity first, service before self, and excellence in all we do. Now I'm convinced that whoever came up with those Air Force core values was reading the Bible. Integrity first, service before self, and then excellence in all that we do are values and expectations that God has for His church.

Arguably, no one can drop a bomb like the US Air Force. Anyone who has ever been in a combat situation and received air support knows exactly what I'm talking about. You don't want the bomber to be average at their job. You don't want mediocrity when an A-10 Warthog comes flying over a tanker unit. you don't want them to be 50% when you're on the ground. Our conduct, or rather, our integrity must be exemplary.

Next, we talked about love and how it is the most important thing. Love is the centerpiece of Paul's exhortation. He makes it clear that without love, it doesn't matter what you do in the church or in the community. If you do it with a spirit of anything other than love, you are nothing more than a clanking symbol. Loveless ministry is just noise. People like this are narcissists trying to be seen.

Then we discussed faith from different aspects, such as having faith in God, and just like y'all have faith in sitting in those chairs, you had faith that those chairs would hold you up, well, our faith in God is that his right hand, according to scripture, will hold us up. We have such confidence in God that we are convinced, and we know that if we don't do what God says, we will fall short of the rewards that come with living a Christian Life of Faith. Again, Paul is telling Timothy that we are to be an example to the believer in all these things.

There are certain things that you don't expect the nonbeliever to do, such as act in love. Secular humanists believe that everything will get better once everybody realizes that all it takes is for people to follow the Golden Rule. Still, over 8,000 years of human history have proven to us that secular humanism is not going to cut it. People have tried to be good, and it hasn't panned out well.

So, we are examples to the Believers, because some people coming after you need to see what a true believer should look like. Some of you reading this book have been in the faith for 30+ years. Others, maybe 30 days or less. Perhaps someone reading a book like this for the first time has not accepted Jesus Christ as their Lord and Savior. I hope something I've written thus far has at least encouraged you to consider following Jesus. This is my personal invitation to you.

To those of us who have accepted Jesus Christ as our Lord and Savior, there is an expectation on your life for you to be an example to others in speech, in conduct, in love, in faith, and here's the big one. Purity. This is one of the hardest. We won't assume that just because it's at the end of Paul's list, that it is of less importance.

As we know, man looks at the outward appearance, but God looks at those things we cannot see. More specifically, God looks at the heart. Scripture teaches that if any man is going to come to God, he must first have clean hands and a pure heart. It almost seems he could have left it with clean hands because ceremonially clean hands make you acceptable to do religious duty. But it is deeper than that.

Let's say I pay my tithes, give to the poor, volunteer at church, and reach out to the community. I make a difference. I typically read my Bible every day. In short, I do all the religious stuff to ensure clean hands, but the question at the end of the day is, what is my motive? The answer to this question requires maturity and a healthy self-image. I argue that there are things that we know deep down inside that we will never admit out loud. We think it, but we don't say it because we know it's not right.

So once you've finished this book, I invite you to ask yourself the tough questions. What is your motive for doing what you do? What is your motive for coming to church? The religious answer might be that you go to church to worship God. You might say you attend services to learn about God so that you can go out and make a difference in the community. Perhaps that is true.

Still, there may be an equivalent truth that motivates us. Maybe we are not aware that some of us go to church because our friends are there. Some go for the inexpensive live entertainment. Many pastors are borderline stand-up comedians these days, and we need something to laugh at or somebody to gossip about. So, if we are honest, maybe we don't really come to church because we're trying to get closer to Jesus.

It is my custom to give a disclaimer at the beginning of all of my sermons to let the hearer know that the congregation is not here to judge or condemn them, but our hope and prayer is that they would hear, see, or experience something that will draw them closer to Jesus Christ. The crazy thing about giving that disclaimer is that some of the most seasoned Christians fall asleep before I finish those words. I guess it is because they've heard them before. My heart breaks for people who ignore vital information simply because they've heard it before. I don't believe it matters how many times we hear the truth if we're not living it.

For instance, who cares how many times you've heard John 3:16 quoted if you still haven't received the finished works of Jesus Christ on the cross? It doesn't matter that you can quote all of Psalm 123. What is your motive for the quote? It seems easy enough to do the religious thing and feel like we're pure before God, but God is looking at our hearts. Like a surgeon, he's looking deep inside, and he wants to know that you know why you do what you do. Why do you really want to preach or sing on the worship team?

Is it because you need to be recognized as a leader in some capacity? I've learned that some people aren't leading at home or on the job, and the only place they can find a sense of validation, a leadership position, or a fancy title is at church. So they come to church, not for God, nor to humble themselves in prayer, nor to help other people through service, but to be lifted up.

The problem with that is that Jesus said, "If I be lifted up, I will draw all men unto Me, not unto us, but unto Himself." However, some have put themselves in the position of Jesus. They are on a mission to draw people to their leadership, their ideas, and their church, and when it does not go the way they expected, they become angry and frustrated, lashing out at those who choose not to follow them.

The best way to avoid ministry frustration and burnout is to understand your why before you ever start. Why do we really do what we do? Why do we want to be whatever it is that we want to be? You might be asking, "What does God want from me?" The answer to that question might not be as mysterious as some, or should I say, many have made it out to be. I believe we tend to over-complicate the idea of divine purpose.

We often think that God's call for our lives is to work a particular job and earn a specific degree. We pray prayers like, "Well, God, which of these jobs should I take? I don't want to be out of your will." We spiritualize job offers as if the Lord were standing before us with a red-and-blue pill. We fear that picking the wrong pill could lead us down a path of mediocrity, or worse. We believe God will punish us for not being able to read his mind.

Some are afraid of marriage because they think God is testing our motives and challenging our idea of love to expose deeply hidden lust in our hearts. Surely God wants you to be equally yoked. Now that we're on topic, you shouldn't have two or three saved sisters in your life that you are trying to figure out which one to keep. If you are, you're not being led by God at all. Something else is leading you. It might be a spirit, but it is not the Holy Spirit!

I was talking to my father one day, and he asked me how and when I knew my wife was the one. I responded without hesitation, "The day I met her." It's not that difficult. Now, I must confess. I'm not as good as some of you. I wasn't one of those guys who never kissed a girl until I met my wife. That is not my story by any means, but of all the ladies available, there was no longer a real option the moment I laid eyes on Jen. The first time I saw her, I knew I was going to marry that girl. If you insist on making your decisions spiritually, here is my advice: Develop discernment through prayer and studying scripture.

Technically speaking, I am not sure that one could marry the wrong person. The real question is, what do you do with that person, or how do you handle arguments, make decisions, or manage resources with the person you've chosen to spend the rest of your life with? I want to relieve you from some of the unnecessary burdens that you put on yourself. As a pastor and counselor with countless hours of biblical studies and a terminal degree, I want to inform you that God does not care what job you choose as long as it does not dishonor his name.

Here are a few career tips:

A. Stop looking for jobs and start looking for a career

B. If you have an entrepreneurial spirit, start looking at what you can create or improve and turn that into a business.

Let's not beat around the bush. We all want to know what the meaning of life is. What does God want from me, and what is his design for my life? We want to know which career we should pursue and whom we should marry. We take the doctrines of predestination and providence to such extremes that I've heard people say they don't get dressed for work or church until God shows them what to wear. I cannot tell you how late I would be for work regularly if I had to hear from God every day about what to wear.

I imagine some of us would become very judgmental of others if we were to inspect their wardrobes to gauge their godliness. You might look at someone who "power clashes" and determine that they are not of God. If you don't know what power clashing means, then I'm talking to you! I'm joking, of course, to make a point. As my father would say, "Let's not be so heavenly-minded that we are no earthly good." I love how Jesus helps us put things into proper balance in Matthew 6:33, "But seek first his kingdom and his righteousness, and all these things will be given to you as well."

The priority in your life, before anything else, is being right with God. Many have lied to themselves and thought themselves smarter than God. When God gives you a word and you say, "Nah, that ain't God," or "I know God didn't tell me to go talk to that person because I have a reason to hate them for the rest of my life." Perhaps you have someone in mind whom you promised you would never forgive, but God said, "Go forgive them!" What do you do, knowing that Jesus said to seek God's Kingdom and His righteousness first? I once heard Dr. Tony Evans say, "If you don't want God, you don't get His heaven."

If you're worried about being married or single, seek first the kingdom, and the right spouse will follow. Seek the kingdom, then the job, then the position at church, then the anointing and the glory. The kingdom is paramount. Everything else is added. Not sold to you, but given to you also.

People who know that seeking God is a priority live a life that says, "I know I don't deserve this, but God blessed me with it. I know I don't have the credentials. I lack credibility. Technically, I don't have the skillset the opportunity requires, but it was given to me as part of the "as well" promise. When you seek God first, you get the divine "as well" coverage, free of charge. Ask the person who works in a career they didn't go to school for. You may not have known the right people or have the pedigree. Perhaps you have a testimony about the "as well" guarantee that landed you some things you know are not of your doing, and because the blessings of God come without sorrow, you can rest in the "as well" blessing!

Again, I warn against overspiritualizing truth, which might tempt us to neglect our part in all of this. If we are not careful, we will fall into a posture of laziness. We know we're there when we start saying things like, "I'm still waiting to hear from God what he wants me to do," or "God hasn't released me to do this or that." We come up with the most creative ways to say, "I lack the motivation to do my part." When you are ready to move beyond your excuses, read Micah 6:8 until you memorize it.

> **"He has shown you, O mortal, what is good. And what does the Lord require of you? To act justly and to love mercy and to walk humbly with your God."**

This text reminds us that God is in control. That's what worship does. That's what getting in the presence of God does: it reminds you that God is boss. I don't care what shirt you wear that says "boss lady!" Some of you have joint social media accounts, and you think that makes you a power couple. Maybe you are a boss, but God is still in control. Perhaps you really are a power couple, but God is still sovereign.

In case you didn't know, at least two things happen in the presence of God. First, you recognize how Mighty God is. Second, you realize how fragile you are. You can lift as many weights as you like. You can run fast and far. Swim like a fish and win a million medals. Your bank account, portfolio, and investment properties are nothing in comparison to God.

He has shown you, oh mortal, what is good. Now here's the question we want answered: what does the Lord require of me? There are a million scriptures, well, maybe not a million, but at least 20 verses in scripture that tell us what God wants from us. As a counselor, when a client says, "I don't know what God wants from me," what I hear you saying is, "I don't read my Bible, and I want you to give me a shortcut." But, because I love you, I'm going to point you to at least one verse that will help you understand what the Lord requires of you. It really is quite simple. That's one of the things I really love about God. He gives us such simple instructions. You might recall Jesus's answer when asked about the greatest commandment. In case you forgot, here it is.

> **Matthew 22:37-40 "Jesus replied: 'Love the Lord your God with all your heart and with all your soul**

and with all your mind.' This is the first and greatest commandment. And the second is like it: 'Love your neighbor as yourself.' All the Law and the Prophets hang on these two commandments."

That's simple. It's an easy instruction until you remember how some people are hard to love. Can you love them when they are undeserving or ungrateful towards you? Keep in mind that the time to assess how good a Christian you are is not when things are going well. It's easy to say God is faithful when you can see the obvious blessing. When things are going well in life, you don't cuss as much. The real test is how you respond to life and what you think and say about God under pressure.

Let's be honest. It's easy to give 10% when you're all your bills are paid and money is good, but when you're broke, tithing requires faith. On the other hand, if you make $300,000 a year and you are led to give 10%, we're talking $30,000. We think it's easy to be generous when you have a lot, but greed is a sneaky spirit. But I've been poor, and I know it's also difficult to be generous when you don't know where your next meal is coming from. We talk about being good stewards, but how good a steward are you when money is funny? How good a spouse are you when your wife is getting on your nerves or when things are going as well as they used to?

What does the Lord require of you then?

Micah 6:8 "He has shown you, O mortal, what is good. And what does the Lord require of you? To act justly and to love mercy and to walk humbly with your God."

That means act like you got some sense in good times and in bad, if you're angry or happy. God is calling us to do the right thing — to love mercy. To be sure, mercy is giving people what they don't deserve. We give people a piece of our mind when we think they deserve it, but mercy is when you hold your peace. That takes humility.

We know all the church cliches, we say all the churchy stuff. We tell people we are blessed and highly favored and brag about being too blessed to be stressed. We say the right things, even if it means lying to others and even to ourselves. Be honest about where you are and how you are doing physically, emotionally, and spiritually. Let me free you up with this. You can be a preacher and be depressed. You can be a worship leader and still struggle with anxiety.

As the songwriter penned: I've had some good days. I've had some hills to climb... all of my good days outweigh my bad days, so I won't complain.

It's dangerous to pretend we are fine when we are not. I found out a long time ago that when we don't talk things out, we act them out. When we are feeling the pressures of life, we might find ourselves bashing people, being rude, or being mean. Why? Because beneath the facade of perfection lies the spirit of pride. Pride lets you forget that temptation comes in seasons. It's easy to be pious when the devil's not knocking at your door. We're reminded to walk humbly with God.

That requires us to check our motives. If you're walking with God only for what you can get from him, you're only fooling yourself. Before accepting the finished works of Christ, I was speeding on motorcycles, fighting in nightclubs, and doing a lot of other things that were not right with God or wise, even in my own eyes. It wasn't until I landed in jail that, with handcuffs on, I said, "God, if you get me out of this one..." That was my honest prayer. You might know that one. In fact, you may have been saying that to God on repeat for some time now.

That broken record should be testimony enough for you to know how much God loves mercy. I believe his mercy gives us time to become more honest with ourselves as we discover the answer to the question we've been wrestling with this entire chapter. What is your motive? Is it just to get something from God? Is your Christianity just your move to keep out of hell, or are you interested in advancing his kingdom?

You can tell if you're interested in advancing his kingdom by looking around the room the next time you're at church. How many people are there because you brought them? When was the last time you shared your faith? Your motive is revealed by what you do with the Jesus that God gave you. I argue that if you're not advancing God's kingdom by reaching lost souls, you might want to ask yourself what you attend church for.

> Matthew 28:18–20 **"Then Jesus came to them and said, "All authority in heaven and on earth has been given to me. Therefore, go and make disciples of all nations, baptizing them in the name of the Father and of the Son and of the Holy Spirit, and teaching them to obey everything I have commanded you. And surely I am with you always, to the very end of the age."**

If we're not doing that, then we are not doing our part. All we're doing is taking the benefits. We are consumers of the Kingdom. Seriously, ask yourself, what am I doing to add value to the kingdom? I'm not known to be a political preacher, and I won't judge you by your voting history, but I might question the motive behind your vote. Many people are loyal to a particular party, no matter what it does or says. Consider the words of the psalmist:

> Psalm 41:1–6 "Blessed are those who have regard for the weak; the Lord delivers them in times of trouble. The Lord protects and preserves them— they are counted among the blessed in the land— he does not give them over to the desire of their foes. The Lord sustains them on their sickbed and restores them from their bed of illness. I said, "Have mercy on me, Lord; heal me, for I have sinned against you." My enemies say of me in malice, "When will he die and his name perish?" When one of them comes to see

me, he speaks falsely, while his heart gathers slander; then he goes out and spreads it around."

Consider also Psalm 41 and ask yourself, How do we define the weak? They are people who cannot defend themselves. We might include people who are sick and those who are financially insecure. I would add people who are powerless about decisions that affect their neighborhood. God calls those who look out for people without a voice blessed. Indeed, the Lord delivers the weak in times of trouble. There will be a time in each of our lives when we are one of the weak ones, and we are going to expect God to do for us what we wouldn't do for somebody else. There will also be times when we reap according to what we sowed.

The former depends on God's mercy. The latter is the benefit of God's order. What we sow, we reap. In those moments, God says, "I got you" because you protected the little ones and had regard for the weak." If you are going to serve, do so with the right motives. Serve with a pure heart.

1 Samuel 15:22 "But Samuel replied: "Does the Lord delight in burnt offerings and sacrifices as much as in obeying the Lord? To obey is better than sacrifice, and to heed is better than the fat of rams."

I once had a minister come to me and tell me she had a word for the church and wanted to preach. I told her I appreciated the offer, but refused to let her preach. She pushed back and demanded to know why. I told her, "If God gave you a word for this church, as the under-shepherd of this house, I believe he would have told me." She insisted, "I have a word for this church. God told me he gifted me, he gave me this word, and I'm supposed to preach here." Her protest did not change my position. I told her again, "No, thank you. We're good."

Her next response might shock some of you. She said, "I don't understand what the problem is. I give money here!" I thought, "So am I supposed to let anybody who gives to this ministry come up, grab a microphone, and say something whenever they feel like it?" Having enough sense not to say that, I responded, "Thank you so much for your gift. We really appreciate your donations, but we don't buy positions here." I added, "but here's what you can do. You can start attending church regularly and participating in the life of the church. Join a group, volunteer where you are needed, and come with the right attitude. Over time, you're more likely to get an opportunity to speak after showing that you can handle the small things.

Ecclesiastes 12:13 "Now all has been heard; here is the conclusion of the matter: Fear God and keep his commandments, for this is the duty of all mankind."

Notice, there are no age requirements in that verse. Your eye color, hair color, or skin color does not exempt you. It doesn't matter what car you drive, how big or small your house is, or what state you live in. Your spouse or job title has nothing to do with this. The duty of all mankind is to fear God and keep his commandments.

How do I stay pure before God? Fear God and keep his commandments. how do I know what God wants for my life? Fear God, keep His Commandments. Whether you're working a 9-to-5 job or if you own your own business, fear God and keep His Commandments. That's purity, ladies and gentlemen; to do what God would smile on. Jesus told his disciples to keep his commandments as evidence of their love for him.

In every relationship, there are healthy boundaries and protocols. When you cross those boundaries or break those protocols, you cause tension in the relationship. If you love the person, you will do all that's in your power to avoid breaking those protocols. When we see people through the lenses of hate, we devalue the way God sees them. Don't misunderstand. I can love you without being your doormat. My love for you doesn't give you access to abuse me.

A few years ago, I determined to start praying that God would save people who mistreat me not solely for their benefit, but for mine. I believe if they get saved, they won't treat me like an enemy. Their hearts will become pure. They will be transformed. They will begin to think like a believer. They will become followers of Christ. If they are truly saved, a life transformation will be their reality. Thus, it is my duty to set the example to believers in speech, conduct, love, faith, and purity. This is especially necessary for new believers. May my life and yours be a testimony, an example, a model of what true Christianity is about.

These five keys now belong to you.

Bibliography

Adams, Jay E. *The Practical Encyclopedia of Christian Counseling*. LOGOS. Institute for Nouthetic Studies, 2020.

Adeyemo, Tokunboh. *Africa Bible Commentary*. WordAlive Publishers; Zondervan, 2006.

Bailey, Boyd. *Two Minutes in the Bible for Men: A 90-Day Devotional*. Harvest House Publishers, 2016.

Braxton, Brad R. "Galatians." In *True to Our Native Land: An African American New Testament Commentary*. Fortress Press, 2007.

Carnegie, Dale. *How to Win Friends and Influence People*. Kindle. Simon & Schuster, n.d.

Clear, James. *Atomic Habits: An Easy & Proven Way to Build Good Habits & Break Bad Ones*. Avery, 2018.

Clinton, Tim, and John Trent. *The Quick-Reference Guide to Marriage & Family Counseling*. n.d.

Collins, Jim. *Good to Great: Why Some Companies Make the Leap... and Others Don't*. HarperCollins Publishers Inc., 2001.

Garland, David E. *1 Corinthians*. Baker Exegetical Commentary on the New Testament. Baker Academic, 2003.

Horton, Michael S. *The Law of Perfect Freedom: Relating to God and Others through The Ten Commandments*. Moody Publisher, 1993.

Hoyt, Thomas. *True to Our Native Land: An African American New Testament Commentary*. Fortress Press, 2007.

Koteskey, R.L.. “Self-Fulfilling Prophecy.” In *Baker Encyclopedia of Psychology & Counseling*. Baker Books, 1999.

Morris, Leon. *1 Corinthians: An Introduction and Commentary*. Vol. 7. Tyndale New Testament Commentaries. InterVarsity Press, 1985.

Peterson, Eugene H. *The Message: The Bible in Contemporary Language*. NavPress, 2005.

Sproul, R. C. *The Holiness of God*. LOGOS. Tyndale House Publishers, 1993.

Stubbs, Monya, A. *True to Our Native Land: An African American New Testament Commentary*. Fortress Press, 2007.

Washington, Booker T. *Up From Slavery*. Dover Thrift Editions: Black History. Dover Publications, 1995.

Zuck, Roy B. *The Speaker's Quote Book*. Logos Research Edition. Kregel, 2004.

Made in the USA
Monee, IL
27 June 2026

55941573R00075